"With *Making Artisan Cheesecake*, author and chef-instructor Melanie Underwood presents 80 enticing recipes for everyone's favorite dessert. In this wide-ranging, yet clearly presented collection, Underwood shows us just how creative cheesecakes can be with everything from a flan-inspired Brazilian cheesecake to a crème brûlée cheesecake to gluten-free and vegan cheesecakes. This cookbook's inspiring flavors and accessible techniques blow the cheesecake category wide open!"

—CHERYL STERNMAN RULE, author, *Yogurt Culture*

MAKING ARTISAN
CHEESECAKE

EXPERT TECHNIQUES FOR
CLASSIC AND CREATIVE RECIPES

MELANIE UNDERWOOD

Quarry Books
100 Cummings Center, Suite 406L
Beverly, MA 01915

quarrybooks.com • quarryspoon.com

© 2015 by Quarry Books

First published in the United States of America in 2015 by
Quarry Books, a member of
Quarto Publishing Group USA Inc.
100 Cummings Center
Suite 406-L
Beverly, Massachusetts 01915-6101
Telephone: (978) 282-9590
Fax: (978) 283-2742
www.quarrybooks.com
Visit www.QuarrySPOON.com and help us celebrate food and culture one spoonful at a time!

10 9 8 7 6 5 4 3 2 1

ISBN: 978-1-63159-054-2

Digital edition published in 2015
eISBN: 978-1-62788-335-1

Library of Congress Cataloging-in-Publication Data
Underwood, Melanie R.
  Making artisan cheesecake : expert techniques for creating your own
creative and classic recipes / Melanie Underwood.
     pages cm
  Includes index.
  ISBN 978-1-63159-054-2
  1. Cheesecake. I. Title.
  TX773.U44 2015
  641.86'53--dc23
                                                    2015005403

Cover and Book Design: Kathie Alexander
Page Layout: *tabula rasa* graphic design
Photography: Marcus Tullis/marcustullis.com
Food styling: Melanie Underwood and Sharon Gutstadt

Printed in China

This book is dedicated to my mom, Mildred,
who taught me strength, courage, and chutzpah.

Contents

Preface

What I have always loved about baking is the enjoyment and delight on people's faces; whether they are learning a new skill or receiving a baked good, baking makes everyone happy. I also love the creativity and flexibility baking offers. But, as a chef instructor at the Institute of Culinary Education for the past nineteen years, I often hear, "baking isn't creative" or "you have to be so precise in baking."

My goal in writing this book is simple, and it is the same goal I have in teaching: to alleviate fears in baking and help people feel comfortable in changing recipes and bringing their personality to what they bake. Many people want to have a recipe that works and just make it, without thinking of how to change it. The recipes in this book offer that, but for those of you who want to play and develop your own recipes, don't be afraid! My goal is always to write recipes that taste amazing and look gorgeous but are also simple to replicate. Cheesecake is so versatile: It can be served sweet, savory, simple, or special.

There is a mystery around cheesecake that should not be there. Cheesecakes are a wonderful choice to make. They can be made in advance and, more important, they are very impressive! By following a few simple techniques, it is one of the easiest things to make. I hope to share my love of cheesecake through these techniques and recipes.

The Basics:
Equipment, Ingredients,
and Techniques

Essential Equipment

PANS

Whether you choose a springform pan, push pan, or cake pan, your baking pan is the most important tool for making cheesecake. Springform pans come in two pieces, a bottom and a side piece with a latch on the side that is released when you are ready to remove the cake from the pan. Springform pans come in a variety of shapes, including round, square, rectangular, oval, and heart-shaped. They can be made from aluminum, nonstick materials, and silicone, and some even have glass bottoms.

Push pans also are two pieces, with a bottom and a side. A push pan bottom fits inside the side piece and is pushed up when the cake is ready to be removed. Some have a silicone ring around the edge to ensure no leaking. These are usually made from aluminum or nonstick materials.

Cake pans can also be used. The benefit is that these ensure that no water leaks into the cake while baking in a water bath. But, they can be more difficult to remove, as you need to invert the cake pan onto a cardboard cake circle covered in plastic wrap, tap the pan to loosen the cheesecake, and then invert the cake onto a serving plate. I like to wrap the bottom and sides of springform and push pans in foil to help alleviate potential leaks.

OTHER IMPORTANT TOOLS

Digital scale, measuring cups, measuring spoons, liquid measures: Invest in a good-quality small digital scale to measure your cheeses. Measuring cups, measuring spoons, and liquid measures are necessary to have in baking.

Rubber spatula: There is a lot of scraping down the sides of the bowl when making cheesecake; a spatula is a must-have.

Whisk: The perfect tool for combining ingredients, beating eggs. and whipping cream.

Electric mixer: Although not necessary to make cheesecake, an electric mixer makes mixing batters much faster and easier. Either a stand mixer or a handheld mixer will work, but a stand mixer allows you more freedom, as you don't have to hold it while it is mixing.

Roasting pan or baking sheet with rim: You want to have a pan with a least ½ inch (1.3 cm) rim to use for the water bath. Any good-quality baking sheet or roasting pan will do. Make sure it is wide enough to accommodate the circumference of the pan. Almost all recipes in this book use a 10-inch (25 cm) pan.

Small offset spatula: This is a great tool for smoothing out the top of the cheesecake batter, swirling batter, or even making repairs on the sides or top after it is baked.

Cardboard cake circle: You can always serve the cheesecake directly on the bottom of the springform or push pan, but I prefer to put the cheesecake on a cardboard cake circle. Make sure you use a cake circle that fits your cheesecake exactly; if you make a 10-inch (25 cm) cheesecake, you will need a 10-inch (25 cm) cake circle. This makes decorating the sides of the cheesecake easier.

Knives: For cutting cheesecake, the best knife is a long, thin, sharp, straight-sided blade. Place the entire blade under very hot water (alternatively, if you have a deep container, fill it with hot water and dip the blade in this), wipe dry with a kitchen towel, immediately place the knife in the center of the cake, and press all the way down to the crust. Pull the knife straight out and place or dip the blade in hot water, wiping the knife dry and

Having the right tools, including an electric stand mixer, push pan or springform pan, liquid and dry measures, a whisk, and a rubber spatula, will make baking cheesecakes much easier.

repeating this process until you have the cake cut into the number of desired pieces.

Unwaxed dental floss: Dental floss can also be used to cut the cheesecake. You will need a piece about 18 inches (45.7 cm) long. Wrap the ends of the floss around your fingers, hold the floss tight, and slide it down through the middle of the cheesecake; repeat this process until you have the cake cut into the number of desired pieces. If the floss cannot cut through the crust, use a thin, sharp blade and press straight down where the cuts were made, and press through the crust.

Cake/pie server: This is very helpful to take out cut pieces and place on your serving plate.

Essential Ingredients

CHEESES

Note: Make sure all of your ingredients, especially the cheeses, are at room temperature when making the cheesecakes. The exception is heavy cream, which needs to be cold when used for whipped cream.

Whenever I have a choice between full-fat, low-fat, or nonfat dairy products, I always opt for the full-fat version. You will get a better texture and flavor in the cheesecakes.

Cream cheese: Fresh cow's milk cream cheese is a staple in cheesecakes. It is a high-fat cheese made with cream, milk, and lactic acid, usually with added stabilizers and gums. It has a mild, slightly tangy flavor and smooth, creamy, but firm texture. Whipped cream cheese is also available, but should not be substituted in recipes.

Neufchâtel: This fresh cow's milk cheese is a great alternative to cream cheese. Made with milk, cream, and gums, it has one-third less fat than cream cheese. It has a mild flavor and smooth, creamy texture.

Ricotta: This fresh cow's milk cheese made from whey is soft with a creamy texture and slightly sweet flavor.

Cottage cheese: With this fresh milk cheese, the cheese is curdled and slightly drained but some whey is left in. It has a slightly sweet flavor and the texture is creamy, yet lumpy.

Farmer cheese: This fresh milk cheese is made by pressing or straining cottage cheese and adding rennet. The texture is crumbly and dry.

Goat cheese: Made from 100 percent goat's milk, this cheese can be fresh or aged, but for cheesecakes fresh is best. It has a creamy texture and tangy flavor.

Yogurt: This fresh fermented milk product can be made with cow or goat's milk. It has a creamy, smooth, liquid texture. Plain yogurt is best in the recipes.

Quark: This fresh cow's milk cheese is slightly drained and is a bit thicker than yogurt.

Fromage blanc: Made with skim cow's milk, fromage blanc is slightly drained, fat-free, and an alternative to yogurt. It is smooth, creamy, and slightly thicker than yogurt.

Heavy Cream: This cow's milk product has a high butter fat content and a rich flavor.

Mascarpone: A fresh cheese made with cow's cream and citric acid, mascarpone comes in double or triple cream and has a buttery flavor, creamy texture, and high fat content.

Nuts: Many different varieties of nuts can be used to make a vegan cheesecake. Nuts high in fat, such as cashews, pecans, hazelnuts, pine nuts, and macadamia nuts, are best.

Vegan cream cheese: This nondairy version is made with water, vegetable oil, thickeners, and sometimes tofu. Although it tastes very different from dairy cream cheese, it has the same texture and is a great substitute.

Vegan sour cream: This nondairy version is made with water, vegetable oil, thickeners, and sometimes tofu. It is slightly more liquid than dairy sour cream but works equally well.

Tofu: This nondairy product is made from soybeans and water. Silken, firm, and extra-firm textures are available.

Clockwise from bottom left: quark, ricotta, cottage cheese, sour cream, feta, Neufchâtel, and cream cheese.

CRUSTS

Ground nuts: Any type of nut can be used for crusts. Almonds, hazelnuts, walnuts, and pecans are the most common; however, peanuts, pistachios, macadamias, cashews, and pine nuts make spectacular crusts. Look for shelled and blanched nuts for easier preparation. When grinding nuts, take care not to overgrind, as they can become very oily.

Ground cookies: There are many cookies that make great crusts, such as chocolate and vanilla wafers, gingersnaps, graham crackers, and even many gluten-free versions of these. When using cookies as the base, it is important to think about how sweet the cookie tastes. The sweeter the cookie, the less sugar you will want to use for making the crust.

Sugar: Granulated, brown sugar, and coconut sugar work well in all the crusts and can be easily substituted for each other. If you use brown sugar, which has molasses, the taste will be slightly sweeter and more robust. Coconut sugar imparts a nice caramel flavor.

All-purpose flour: This is used in the flaky and sweet dough recipes. If you want to substitute whole-wheat flour in these recipes, use half whole-wheat and half all-purpose.

Eggs: Eggs are used in the sweet dough recipes. They give the dough a tender texture that is more like a cookie.

Butter: This is used to give flavor and provide tenderness and flakiness. For recipes calling for melted butter, any type of liquid fat can be substituted, including nut or vegetable oils. For recipes calling for solid butter, other solid fats, such as solidified coconut oil, leaf lard, or bacon fat, may be used. However, liquid fats should not be substituted for solid fats.

From top, left: ground pistachios, ground chocolate cookies, ground graham crackers; middle: ground almonds, ground hazelnuts, all-purpose flour; bottom: sugar, melted butter, brown sugar, eggs

Simple Ground Crusts

One of my favorite crusts is a simple mixture of ground cookies or nuts (or both), sugar (if desired), and melted butter. I love being able to choose a cookie crust's color and flavor—vanilla or chocolate wafers, gingersnaps, or the classic graham crackers—and modify it by adding other flavors (see chart below). If you'd like to combine cookies and nuts in your crust, use equal amounts of each.

Whether you add sugar is a matter of personal taste, and you can substitute your favorite liquid fat for the melted butter. Coconut and nut oils both add delicious flavors. Typically, ground crusts are baked before the batter is added to the pan; alternatively, they can be frozen for a minimum of 20 minutes.

Ground crusts are the easiest to get into a springform pan. Place the mixture into the pan and, using your palm or the bottom of a glass, press it firmly and evenly into the bottom. If you want crust on the sides of your cheesecake, prepare the larger recipe on page 17, press about half the mixture into the bottom of the pan, then use the sides of a glass to press the rest of the mixture into the sides.

Cookie Crust Variations

Add these flavorings to ground cookie crumbs before adding butter or oil.

	Bottom-only crust	Bottom-and-sides crust
Spiced	1 teaspoon cinnamon	1½ teaspoons cinnamon
Cocoa	2 tablespoons (10 g) cocoa powder	3 tablespoons (16 g) cocoa powder
Citrus	2 teaspoons (4 g) grated lemon or orange zest	1 tablespoon (6 g) grated lemon or orange zest
Almond	2 tablespoons (12 g) finely ground almonds plus 1 teaspoon almond extract	3 tablespoons (18 g) finely ground almonds plus 1½ teaspoons almond extract
Brown sugar	Use light or dark brown sugar instead of granulated sugar.	

BOTTOM-ONLY COOKIE CRUST

1¾ cups (205 g) finely ground cookie crumbs (about 10 graham crackers or 32 vanilla wafers, chocolate wafers, or gingersnaps)

2 tablespoons (26 g) sugar

8 tablespoons (112 g) unsalted butter, melted

BOTTOM-AND-SIDES COOKIE CRUST

2⅔ cups (304 g) finely ground cookie crumbs (about 15 graham crackers or 48 vanilla wafers, chocolate wafers, or gingersnaps)

3 tablespoons (39 g) sugar

12 tablespoons (168 g) unsalted butter, melted

BOTTOM-ONLY NUT CRUST

2 cups (190 g) finely ground nuts (such as almonds, walnuts, or pecans; mix no more than two)

2 tablespoons (26 g) granulated or brown sugar

3 tablespoons (42 g) unsalted butter, melted

Preheat the oven to 350°F (180°C, or gas mark 4).

In a medium bowl, combine the ground cookies or nuts and sugar. Add the butter and stir with a rubber spatula to combine, making sure all the butter is absorbed and the crumbs or nuts are evenly coated.

Place the mixture in a 10-inch (25 cm) springform pan. Using the palm of your hand or the bottom of a glass, press the mixture firmly into the bottom of the pan. For a bottom-and-sides crust, use the sides of a glass to press about half of the mixture into the sides of the pan.

Place the pan in the oven and bake for about 10 minutes, or until slightly firm. (The nut crust will be toasted to a golden brown and have a nutty aroma.) Remove from the oven and allow to cool completely, about 10 minutes.

GRAHAM CRACKER–PEANUT BUTTER CRUST

1 cup (120 g) graham cracker crumbs

2 tablespoons (32 g) peanut butter

1 tablespoon (4 g) unsalted butter

Preheat the oven to 350°F (180°C, or gas mark 4).

In a medium bowl, combine the ground graham crackers and peanut butter. Add the butter and stir with a rubber spatula to combine, making sure all the butter is absorbed and the crumbs are evenly coated.

Place the mixture in a 10-inch (25 cm) springform pan. Using the palm of your hand or the bottom of a glass, press the mixture firmly into the bottom of the pan.

Place the pan in the oven and bake for about 10 minutes, or until slightly firm. Remove from the oven and allow to cool completely, about 10 minutes.

Cake and Brownie Crusts

Cake and brownie bases are a wonderful change from the usual crust and make for an impressive cheesecake. When using a cake or brownie base for your cheesecake, you can bake it right in the springform pan. If you want to prepare the crust in advance, you can bake it in a separate cake or brownie pan and trim it to fit the springform. Regardless of which pan you bake it in, you'll need to brush the bottom and sides of the pan with melted butter, and then lightly coat it with flour before adding the cake batter and baking according to the recipe instructions. It is important in making the cake and brownie crusts that all ingredients be at room temperature.

REMOVING A CAKE OR BROWNIE CRUST FROM THE PAN

If you bake a cake or brownie crust in a traditional cake pan, make sure the pan is the same size or slightly larger than your springform, and let the crust cool before attempting to remove it from the pan.

The best way to remove a cake crust is to loosen it by running a small knife around its edges, placing a cardboard cake circle on top of it, and then inverting it onto the cardboard. If the crust won't slip out easily, try loosening it by lightly tapping the pan on a hard surface.

Once the crust has been removed, place the bottom of the springform pan on top of the cake. Using a small knife, saw back and forth to trim the crust to the springform bottom's shape so it will fit perfectly in the pan. Place the crust back on the cardboard circle, insert the springform bottom back into the pan, and then slide the crust off the cardboard into the springform. The crust is now ready to be topped with cheesecake batter.

LEMON CAKE CRUST

1½ cups (188 g) all-purpose flour

¼ teaspoon baking soda

Pinch of salt

½ cup (112 g) unsalted butter, at room temperature, cut into 1-inch (2.5 cm) pieces

1 cup (200 g) sugar

2 large eggs

½ cup (120 ml) buttermilk

2 tablespoons (30 ml) lemon juice

1 tablespoon (6 g) lemon zest

Preheat the oven to 350ºF (180ºC, or gas mark 4). Brush melted butter on the bottom and sides of a 10- or 12-inch (25 or 30.5 cm) cake pan. Lightly flour, rotating the pan to cover the bottom and sides completely, and then knock out the excess. Set aside.

In a large bowl, whisk together the flour, baking soda, and salt; set aside.

In the bowl of an electric mixer, using the paddle attachment, cream the butter and sugar together until light and fluffy, about 5 minutes. Beat in the eggs, one at a time, scraping down the sides of the bowl occasionally.

With the mixer off, stir one-third of the dry ingredients into the egg mixture, and then mix on low speed for about 1 minute. Add half of the buttermilk and stir. Add another third of the dry ingredients and then add the remaining half of the buttermilk mixture, scraping the bowl with a rubber spatula. Add the remaining dry ingredients. Stir in the lemon juice and zest.

Pour the batter into the prepared pan and bake until the cake springs back when touched in the center or a toothpick inserted comes out clean, about 20 minutes. Remove from the oven and allow to cool completely before adding the batter or, if a separate cake pan was used, before attempting to remove the cake from the pan.

RED VELVET CAKE CRUST

4 tablespoons (56 g) unsalted butter, at room temperature, cut into 1-inch (2.5 cm) pieces

½ cup (100 g) granulated sugar

¼ cup (60 g) packed light brown sugar

Pinch of sea salt

1 tablespoon (15 ml) vanilla extract

2 large egg yolks

2 tablespoons (28 ml) liquid red food coloring

2 tablespoons (14 g) cocoa powder

1 cup (125 g) all-purpose flour

½ cup (120 ml) buttermilk

2 teaspoons (10 ml) white vinegar

½ teaspoon (2.3 g) baking soda

Preheat the oven to 350°F (180°C, or gas mark 4). Brush a 10-inch (25 cm) springform pan with melted butter. Lightly flour, rotating the pan to cover the bottom and sides completely, and then knock out the excess. Set aside.

In the bowl of an electric mixer using the paddle attachment, combine the butter and the granulated sugar, brown sugar, salt, and vanilla extract; mix on medium speed until light and fluffy, about 10 minutes. The mixture should look very light and grainy. Turn the mixer off and use a rubber spatula to scrape down the sides of the bowl; add the egg yolks and mix well until combined, about 1 minute.

In a small bowl, whisk together the food coloring and cocoa powder and stir into the egg mixture just until combined, about 1 minute. Turn the mixer off and scrape down the sides of the bowl, underneath the paddle, and the paddle.

Add half of the flour and mix on low speed to combine, about 1 minute, just until the flour is absorbed. Slowly add all the buttermilk and mix for 1 minute. Turn the mixer off, scrape down the sides of the bowl, and then add the remaining flour; mix on low just until combined.

In a small bowl, combine the vinegar and baking soda; immediately add to the cake batter and stir, by hand, using a rubber spatula, just until combined. Pour the batter into the springform pan and bake for 18 to 20 minutes, or until the cake springs back when touched or a toothpick inserted into the center of the cake comes out clean or with crumbs, but no wet batter. Remove from the oven and allow to cool completely before adding the batter, or if a separate cake pan was used, before attempting to remove the cake from the pan.

Once a cake or brownie crust that's been baked separately has been removed from the pan, place the bottom of the springform pan on top of it, and then use a small knife to trim the crust to its shape, sawing back and forth as you go. Place the cake circle back on the cardboard, insert the pan bottom back into the springform, then slide the trimmed crust off the cardboard and into the springform.

Cake and Brownie Crusts *(continued)*

CARROT CAKE CRUST

¼ cup (60 ml) large eggs

½ cup (115 g) light brown sugar

5 tablespoons (75 ml) grapeseed or other vegetable oil

2 tablespoons (28 ml) milk

¼ cup (31 g) whole-wheat flour

¼ cup (31 g) all-purpose flour

1 tablespoon (7 g) ground flaxseed

½ teaspoon baking powder

⅛ teaspoon baking soda

⅛ teaspoon ground cinnamon

¾ cup (83 g) grated carrot

¼ cup (30 g) finely chopped walnuts (optional)

Preheat the oven to 350ºF (180ºC, or gas mark 4). Brush a 10-inch (25 cm) springform pan with melted butter. Set aside.

In a medium-size bowl, whisk together the eggs, brown sugar, oil, and milk until combined. Set aside.

In another bowl, whisk together the whole-wheat flour, all-purpose flour, flaxseed, baking powder, baking soda, and cinnamon.

Pour the egg mixture into the dry ingredients; add the carrots and nuts and stir until combined. Pour the batter into the springform pan and bake for 18 to 20 minutes, or until the cake springs back when touched or a toothpick inserted into the center of the cake comes out clean or with crumbs, but no wet batter. Remove from the oven and allow to cool completely before adding the batter, or if a separate cake pan was used, before attempting to remove the cake from the pan.

BROWNIE CRUST

4 tablespoons (56 g) unsalted butter, cut into 1-inch (2.5 cm) pieces

4 ounces (112 g) semisweet chocolate, finely chopped

2 large eggs

½ cup (100 g) sugar

1 teaspoon vanilla extract

2 tablespoons (10 g) cocoa powder, sifted

6 tablespoons (48 g) all-purpose flour

½ teaspoon baking powder

Preheat the oven to 350ºF (180ºC, or gas mark 4).

In a medium-size bowl, combine the butter and chocolate. Place over a double boiler and stir until melted. Remove from the heat and allow to cool slightly.

In another medium-size bowl, whisk together the eggs, sugar, and vanilla until lightened in color, about 3 minutes. Whisk the egg mixture into the cooled chocolate mixture. Add the cocoa, flour, and baking powder and stir until combined.

Pour batter into the springform pan and bake for 12 to 15 minutes, or until the brownie springs back when touched or a toothpick inserted into the center out clean, with no wet batter. Remove from the oven and allow to cool completely before adding the batter, or if a separate cake pan was used, before attempting to remove the cake from the pan.

VARIATION

To make Espresso Brownie Crust, make Brownie Crust, but add 1 tablespoon (8 g) of instant espresso powder to the melted butter and chocolate.

Pastry and Flaky Crusts

Pastry and flaky crusts are perfect if you prefer a heartier crust. I like to use these for the savory cheesecakes for the perfect textural balance. The recipes shown here are to be made in a food processor, but all of these doughs can also be made by hand. The only difference is that when adding the butter, you should use your fingertips or a pastry blender to incorporate. Although these crusts are traditionally rolled out with a rolling pin, these recipes can also be pressed in by hand, which saves time and energy. If you do prefer rolling out the dough, be sure to chill the dough for at least 1 hour before rolling. For pastry and flaky crusts, make sure all ingredients are chilled.

FLAKY DOUGH CRUST

1¼ cups (156 g) all-purpose flour

1 tablespoon (15 g) sugar (optional)

½ teaspoon salt

½ cup (115 g) cold unsalted butter, cut into 1-inch (2.5 cm) pieces

3 to 4 tablespoons (45 to 60 ml) ice water

Preheat the oven to 350°F (180°C, or gas mark 4).

In the bowl of a food processor, combine the flour, sugar, and salt. Pulse once or twice to mix completely. Add the butter and pulse into the dry ingredients until the mixture resembles a coarse ground cornmeal and no large pieces of butter remain visible. Add 3 tablespoons (45 ml) of ice water and pulse just until the mixture comes together (if you pinch a small piece of dough, it will easily hold together). If it is not easily holding together, continue to add more of the remaining 1 tablespoon (15 ml) water.

Remove from the food processor. Using your fingers, pinch off small pieces of dough and place them all over the bottom of a 10-inch (25 cm) springform pan. Using the palm of your hand or the bottom of a glass, press the dough evenly into the bottom of the pan. Chill for 30 minutes. Place the pan in the oven and bake for 18 to 20 minutes, or until lightly golden and firm, but not hard to the touch. Remove from the oven and allow to cool completely.

VARIATIONS

Chocolate Flaky Dough Crust: Reduce the flour to 1⅛ cups (141 g) and add 2 tablespoons (10 g) cocoa powder to the dry ingredients.

Cornmeal Flaky Dough Crust: Reduce the flour to 1⅛ cups (141 g) and add 2 tablespoons (18 g) cornmeal to the dry ingredients.

Incorporate the cold butter by hand. Gently flatten it between your thumbs and first two fingers until only small pieces remain.

Drizzle in the cold water, stirring with a rubber spatula until the dough holds together, being careful not to overwork it.

To press the dough into the cheesecake pan, use your hand or the bottom of a glass and press evenly.

Pastry and Flaky Crusts *(continued)*

SWEET DOUGH CRUST

2 cups (250 g) all-purpose flour

3 tablespoons (39 g) sugar

Pinch of sea salt

6 tablespoons (85 g) cold unsalted butter,
  cut into 1-inch (2.5 cm) pieces

2 large eggs

2 large egg yolks

Preheat the oven to 350°F (180°C, or gas mark 4).

In the bowl of a food processor, combine the flour, sugar, and salt. Pulse once or twice to mix completely. Add the butter and pulse into the dry ingredients until the mixture resembles a fine ground cornmeal and no pieces of butter remain visible. Whisk the eggs and yolks together in a small bowl and add to the flour and butter mixture. Pulse this just until the mixture is uniform in color and comes together (if you pinch a small piece of dough, it will easily hold together). Remove from the food processor.

Using your fingers, pinch off small pieces of dough and place them all over the bottom of a 10-inch (25 cm) springform pan. Using the palm of your hand or the bottom of a glass, press the dough evenly into the bottom of the pan. Place the pan in the oven and bake the crust for 18 to 20 minutes, or until lightly golden and firm, but not hard to the touch. Remove from the oven and allow to cool completely.

CREAM CHEESE CRUST

1¼ cups (156 g) all-purpose flour

½ teaspoon salt

3 ounces (85 g) cold unsalted butter,
  cut into 1-inch (2.5 cm) pieces

3 ounces (85 g) cold cream cheese,
  cut into cubes

2 tablespoons (30 ml) heavy cream

Preheat the oven to 350°F (180°C, or gas mark 4).

In the bowl of a food processor, combine the flour and salt. Pulse once or twice to mix completely.

Add the butter and cream cheese and pulse into the dry ingredients until the mixture resembles a coarse ground cornmeal and no pieces of butter or cream cheese remain visible. Add the heavy cream and pulse just until the mixture is uniform in color and comes together (if you pinch a small piece of dough, it will easily hold together). Remove from the food processor.

Using your fingers, pinch off small pieces of dough and place them all over the bottom of a 10-inch (25 cm) springform pan. Using the palm of your hand or the bottom of a glass, press the dough evenly into the bottom of the pan. Place the pan in the oven and bake the crust for 18 to 20 minutes, or until lightly golden and firm, but not hard to the touch. Remove from the oven and allow to cool completely.

VARIATIONS

Nut Sweet Dough Crust: *Add 2 tablespoons (10 g) ground nuts to the dry ingredients.*

Chocolate Sweet Dough Crust: *Reduce the flour to 1⅛ cups (141 g) and add 2 tablespoons (10 g) cocoa powder to the dry ingredients.*

Sesame Seed Sweet Dough Crust: *Add ¼ cup (36 g) black sesame seeds to the dry ingredients.*

Other Types of Crusts

PARMESAN AND HERB CRUST

This savory pastry crust is so versatile, you can substitute other hard cheeses and any kind or herbs.

1¼ cups (156 g) all-purpose flour

2 tablespoons (13 g) finely grated Parmesan

2 tablespoons (6 g) finely chopped chives

½ teaspoon sea salt

½ cup (112 g) cold unsalted butter, cut into 1-inch (2.5 cm) pieces

2 large egg yolks

2 tablespoons (30 ml) cold water

Preheat the oven to 350ºF (180ºC, or gas mark 4).

In the bowl of a food processor, combine the flour, Parmesan, chives, and salt. Pulse once or twice to mix completely. Pulse the butter into the dry ingredients until the mixture resembles a coarse ground cornmeal and no pieces of butter remain visible. Whisk the egg yolks and water together in a small bowl and add to the flour and butter mixture. Pulse just until the mixture is uniform in color and comes together (if you pinch a small piece of dough, it will easily hold together). Remove from the food processor.

Using your fingers, pinch off small pieces of dough and place them all over the bottom of a 10-inch (25 cm) springform or cake pan. Using the palm of your hand or the bottom of a glass, press the dough evenly into the bottom of the pan. Place the pan in the oven and bake the crust for 18 to 20 minutes, or until lightly golden and firm, but not hard to the touch. Remove from the oven and allow to cool completely.

VARIATION

Substitute any type of hard cheese or any type of herb.

BACON CRUST

1¼ cups (156 g) all-purpose flour

¼ cup (20 g) crumbled cooked bacon

½ teaspoon salt

4 ounces (112 g) solidified bacon fat

3 to 4 tablespoons (45 to 60 ml) ice water

Preheat the oven to 350ºF (180ºC, or gas mark 4).

In the bowl of a food processor, combine the flour, bacon, and salt. Pulse once or twice to mix.

Add the bacon fat and pulse into the dry ingredients until the mixture resembles ground cornmeal and the fat is incorporated. Add 3 tablespoons (45 ml) of the water and pulse until the mixture comes together (if you pinch a small piece of dough, it will hold together). If not, add the remaining 1 tablespoon (15 ml) water. Set the dough aside.

Using your fingers, pinch off small pieces of dough and place them all over the bottom of a 10-inch (25 cm) springform pan. Using the palm of your hand or the bottom of a glass, press the dough evenly into the bottom of the pan. Place the pan in the oven and bake the crust for 18 to 20 minutes, or until lightly golden and firm, but not hard to the touch. Remove from the oven and allow to cool completely.

Note: To roll out dough, refrigerate for at least 1 hour before rolling. Place a piece of parchment paper on a work surface and dust with all-purpose flour. Place the dough on the parchment and then lightly dust with more flour. Begin rolling the dough with the rolling pin directly in front of you and roll away from you applying even pressure. Rotate the dough one-eighth and repeat this process until the dough is about ¼-inch (6 mm) thick and 10 to 11 inches (25 to 28 cm) across. Trim the dough to fit inside the pan. Bake as directed.

Other Types of Crusts *(continued)*

These crusts are called for in specific recipes, but they can be used in many of them. The crumb crust is an excellent choice if you want a sweeter, richer crust. The sweet potato crust can be used for any savory recipe and has beautiful color and a wonderful crunchy texture.

STREUSEL CRUMB CRUST

This makes enough for the crust and topping for the Caramel Apple Crumb Cheesecake (page 70). If using just for a crust, reduce the mixture by one-third.

3 cups (375 g) all-purpose flour

1½ cups (340 g) light brown sugar

¾ cup (60 g) rolled oats

1 tablespoon (7 g) ground cinnamon

Pinch of ground nutmeg

12 ounces (337 g) unsalted butter, melted

Preheat the oven to 350°F (180°C, or gas mark 4).

In a large bowl, combine the flour, brown sugar, oats, cinnamon, and nutmeg. Add the butter all at once and stir until completely combined and the mixture begins to come together.

Remove two-thirds of the streusel and press it into the bottom of a springform pan. Set aside the remaining one-third for the topping. Place in the oven and bake for 18 to 20 minutes, or until formed and lightly golden. Remove from the oven and allow to cool completely.

VEGAN COCONUT CRUST

1½ cups (188 g) all-purpose flour

2 tablespoons (18 g) coconut or granulated sugar

4 ounces (112 g) cold coconut butter

½ cup (120 ml) cold water

Preheat the oven to 350°F (180°C, or gas mark 4).

In the bowl of a food processor, combine the flour and sugar. Pulse once or twice to mix completely. Pulse the coconut butter into the dry ingredients until it is completely mixed and no pieces remain visible. Add ¼ cup (60 ml) of the water and pulse to combine; add the remaining ¼ cup (60 ml) water and pulse again until completely combined and uniform in color. Remove from the food processor.

Using your fingers, pinch off small pieces of dough and place them all over the bottom of a 10-inch (25 cm) springform or cake pan. Using the palm of your hand or the bottom of a glass, press the dough evenly into the bottom of the pan. Place the pan in the oven and bake the crust for 18 to 20 minutes, or until lightly golden and firm, but not hard to the touch. Remove from the oven and allow to cool completely.

GRATED SWEET POTATO OR POTATO CRUST

This is a beautiful and unusual crust to substitute for any of the savory crusts.

2 pounds (908 g) sweet potatoes or potatoes, peeled and coarsely grated on a box grater

1 tablespoon (19 g) kosher salt

1 tablespoon (8 g) all-purpose flour

1 large egg

½ teaspoon ground black pepper

1 tablespoon (15 ml) grapeseed oil or melted unsalted butter

Toss together the sweet potatoes and salt and place in a colander. Allow to drain for 30 minutes.

Preheat the oven to 400°F (200°C, or gas mark 6).

Remove the sweet potatoes from the colander; place in a kitchen towel and squeeze to remove all excess water. Transfer to a bowl; add the flour, egg, and pepper and toss to combine.

Brush the oil on the sides and bottom of a 10-inch (25 cm) springform pan. Pour the sweet potatoes into the pan and press into a thin layer on the bottom and sides. Place in the oven and bake for 20 to 25 minutes, or until firm and lightly golden. Remove from the oven and allow to cool completely.

Batters

Far left: After the cream cheese is smooth and creamy, and no lumps are visible, gradually add the sugar in a slow, steady steam.

Left: Once the sugar has been completely mixed in, add the eggs one at a time, mixing for about 20 seconds after each addition. Use a rubber spatula to scrape down the sides of the bowl and underneath the paddle after each egg has been incorporated.

BASIC CHEESECAKE BATTERS

Basic batters consist of fresh, soft cheeses; sugar; eggs; flavoring; and sometimes starch, such as flour or cornstarch. These are generally baked on a pastry or ground cookie crust. You can substitute ingredients, but you need to use ingredients that have a similar texture and consistency. I recommend that when substituting ingredients, you only change one at a time so you know how it will alter the recipe. If you substitute multiple ingredients, you will not know what caused the change in the final cake. Starch can be omitted from the cheesecake recipes, but the baking time will be longer and the texture slightly lighter.

All ingredients in any cheesecake batter need to be at room temperature for at least 2 hours before mixing. Using cold ingredients can cause the batter to have lumps of cheese that will remain after baked. Also, if using cold ingredients, you will have to beat the mixture more to work out the lumps, which will over aerate the cheesecake and cause cracking.

When mixing the batter, the speed on the mixer should be medium to medium-low, so as not to over aerate. Using a rubber spatula, frequently scrape down the sides of the bowl to help prevent lumps. An alternative to using a mixer is to use a food processor with the metal blade, being careful to just pulse until the ingredients are combined. If you opt to use a food processor, you can follow the recipe as written.

Batters *(continued)*

SOUFFLÉ–STYLE CHEESECAKE BATTERS

These batters are made like a basic batter, but with the addition of whipped egg whites for a lighter texture. Properly whipped whites and proper folding technique are essential to the success of these cheesecakes. Start with room temperature egg whites; beat with a whisk attachment with either an electric or a handheld mixer on medium speed until very frothy, and then increase the speed to medium-high. Egg whites should be stiff but glossy when properly whipped. Caution: If they looked glossy, but then become grainy, they are over whipped.

For folding, take one-eighth of the beaten egg whites and add to the initial cheesecake mixture, and then whisk or stir with a rubber spatula until completely combined. This will lighten the texture of the batter. When the batter is a similar consistency as the egg whites, folding is more successful and it is less likely the whites will be overworked. Using a large rubber spatula, add in half of the remaining egg whites and fold in: Cut down the center of the mixture with the wide side of the spatula, lift the mixture up, and turn over, as if you are making the letter J. Rotate the bowl 90 degrees and repeat one more time. Add in the remaining egg whites and continue folding until the egg whites are just fully incorporated. Do not continue mixing once the egg whites are completely incorporated, as the mixture will deflate and become dense.

Add one-eighth of the glossy, stiff egg whites to the batter and stir until the egg whites are completely combined.

Fold in the egg whites: Using the wide side of a large rubber spatula, cut down the center of the bowl, lift the mixture up, and turn the spatula over. Rotate the bowl one-quarter turn every time you fold, as if you are making the letter J.

Add the remaining egg whites and continue folding as above. Continue until no streaks of egg white remain.

NO-BAKE CHEESECAKE BATTERS

These simple cheesecakes have no eggs or starch and require no baking. Some no-bake cheesecakes are set with gelatin and others are not. The texture is generally lighter than a baked cheesecake. These are very creative and perfect for serving in individual portions. It is a great choice in the summertime if you don't want to turn on the oven.

Granulated gelatin that has been bloomed in cool water, to be placed over a double boiler and melted

Placing sheet gelatin in a bowl of cold water to soften

Decorative Techniques

Once the batters are fully chilled, place the bottom layer of batter in the springform pan. Carefully spread it with a small offset spatula to smooth its surface and make it level. Very gently dollop the second batter onto the first and, using a small offset spatula, spread it evenly.

LAYERING BATTERS

A layered cheesecake looks stunning when sliced, and is so simple to achieve. The best batters for this effect are thicker, meaning that they're spreadable rather than pourable. My favorite way to do this—working with fully chilled batters—requires a couple of hours of additional time, and consequently some advance planning, but the reaction of anyone who is served a slice will be well worth it.

After you've prepared your batters, refrigerate them until they're thoroughly chilled, which usually takes 2 to 3 hours. You can use the layering technique shown above even if you don't have time to chill your batters, but the top batter may sink slightly into the bottom one. The cheesecake may not have two even layers, but it will still be beautiful.

Place your batters in the springform pan using one of the two methods described. Use a knife or small spatula to gently swirl C or L shapes on the surface, taking care to avoid the crust.

SWIRLING BATTERS

Swirling two or more batters or fillings together is an easy way to give a cheesecake an elegant finish without having to do a lot of garnishing or decorating. There are two ways to prepare the batters in order to achieve a swirled effect.

Method 1: Level the first batter on top of a prepared crust using a small offset spatula. Using 1 cup (240 g) of the second batter, gently place small dollops ¼ inch (6 mm) apart on the first batter's surface.

Method 2: Create three layers of batter by pouring and leveling half of the first, all of the second, then the remaining half of the first.

Use a knife or a small spatula to make C or L shapes in the batter, taking care not to touch the crust. You can swirl the batters as much as you like, but if you overswirl them you may lose the effect.

Baking and Cooking Methods

Basic batters are best baked in a water bath, using a rimmed sheet tray, a roasting pan, or even a large (14-inch [35.6 cm]) cake pan. A water bath helps maintain a smooth texture and prevents overbaking and cracking. Some recipes will call for a covered water bath, but I prefer to leave mine uncovered. If you are using a springform pan, you will want to wrap the outside of the pan in foil. This can also be done if you are using a push pan, but it is not required. If you do not have an 18-inch (45.7 cm)-wide roll of foil, then first wrap the pan in plastic wrap coming up almost to the top of the pan, then wrap in two layers of foil, coming almost to the top of the pan. If you have a large roll, one layer of foil will work. This prevents water from seeping into the bottom of the pan and making the crust soggy.

Place the springform pan in a large cake pan or a roasting pan (one that is around the same height or lower than your springform pan). Pour the batter over the crust and level it with a small offset spatula. Place the roasting pan with the cheesecake in the oven and pour almost boiling water into the roasting pan (the water should come up halfway around the sides of the springform pan).

When it is finished baking, remove the entire tray from the oven, then remove the cheesecake from the water bath. Remove the foil from the sides of the pan.

An alternative to placing directly in a water bath is to place your cheesecake on the top rack of the oven and a tray with water on the lower rack. If you choose this method, you can skip wrapping the pan. Of course, you can bake without any steam in the oven at all. Simply put the cheesecake on a baking tray and place it directly in your oven. I prefer the water bath because the texture is creamy and smooth, and can prevent the top from cracking. If you prefer a drier texture for the cheesecake, omit the water bath.

Cheesecakes are generally baked at 325ºF (170ºC, or gas mark 3) until almost set. They will appear slightly jiggly in the center, but will continue to set once they are removed from the oven and are chilled. Cooking longer will produce a dry, overcooked cheesecake. Once it is removed from the oven, run a paring knife around the edges of the cheesecake to loosen the edges from the pan, as this will also help prevent cracking. Allow to cool at room temperature, and then place in the refrigerator for at least 8 hours (this will help the cheesecake set completely).

REMOVING A CHEESECAKE FROM THE PAN

You have to decide whether you want to serve your cheesecake directly on the bottom of your pan or transfer it to a cardboard cake circle. Leaving it on the bottom of the pan is fine, but keep in my mind that you will see the metal when serving it whole. This is the easiest method.

A hot water bath, also known as a bain marie, helps keep the cheesecake moist, keeps the texture smooth, and prevents over baking and cracking. Make sure your springform pan is wrapped well with foil and placed in a roasting pan. The roasting pan will be placed in the oven and then filled halfway with very hot water.

A covered water bath is another technique that keeps cheesecake smooth and prevents cracking. Wrap the springform pan well in foil and place in a roasting pan, add ½ to 1 cup (120 to 235 ml) water to the roasting pan, and cover the entire roasting pan tightly with foil.

Before unmolding any cheesecake, gently run a small knife or an offset spatula around the edges of the cheesecake to loosen them. If using a springform pan, unlatch the latch on the side of the pan and simply remove the side, lifting it straight up. If you are using a push pan, place the push pan on a can or a small bowl and push down on the sides of the pan. You can also purchase a special stand made specifically for this purpose.

At that point, if you want to transfer it to a cardboard cake circle or directly onto the serving platter, you will need two cardboard circles, with one wrapped in plastic wrap. Place the cardboard wrapped in plastic wrap on top of the cheesecake and invert the cheesecake, then loosen the bottom of the pan that is still on the cheesecake. Gently remove the bottom of the pan and place the other piece of cardboard on the bottom; invert the cheesecake back and then gently remove the cardboard covered in plastic wrap from the top of the cheesecake.

STORING, FREEZING, AND THAWING

Once cheesecakes are completely set and have been chilled in the refrigerator, place on a cardboard cake circle, wrap in plastic wrap, and store in the refrigerator. Although cheesecakes will last for 5 to 7 days in the refrigerator, I prefer to keep them only 2 or 3 days. After that, the crust becomes wet and soggy and loses its texture. Cheesecakes that are stored improperly will dry out, crack, and become hard around the edges and sides.

If you have leftovers or want to make a cheesecake in advance, it can be frozen for 6 months without a change in texture. Double wrap tightly in plastic wrap and then wrap in foil. To defrost, place the cheesecake in the refrigerator 24 hours before you want to serve it. Unwrap the foil and plastic wrap and serve.

All cheesecakes should be garnished or decorated after being defrosted.

Classic
Cheesecakes

Although these classic cheesecakes are simple,
they are full of flavor. These are the perfect basics
to experiment with and develop your own flavors.

New York–Style Cheesecake

This delicious, creamy classic, which features a flaky crust (page 21), is adapted from one of fellow instructor Nick Malgieri's recipes in his "Introduction to Baking and Pastry" class.

CRUST
Flaky Dough Crust (page 21)

CHEESECAKE
1 pound (454 g) cream cheese

1 cup (200 g) sugar

2 cups (460 g) sour cream

4 large eggs

1 teaspoon vanilla extract

To make the crust: Preheat the oven to 350ºF (180ºC, or gas mark 4). Follow the instructions on page 21 for the Flaky Dough Crust. Let cool completely before adding the cheesecake batter.

To make the cheesecake: Lower the oven temperature to 325ºF (170ºC, or gas mark 3).

In the bowl of an electric mixer, using the paddle attachment, mix the cream cheese on low speed until softened, scraping down the sides of the bowl, underneath the paddle, and the paddle frequently with a rubber spatula, about 2 minutes. Add the sugar and continue mixing on low and scraping down the sides, bottom, and paddle until there are no visible lumps. Add the sour cream and mix just until combined. Add the eggs, one at a time, and mix just until combined, about 10 seconds after each egg. Stir in the vanilla extract.

Prepare the springform pan for a water bath (see page 30). Pour the batter over the prepared crust and spread it evenly with a small offset spatula. Set the springform pan in a roasting pan and prepare the water bath as directed. Bake for about 1 hour, or until the cheesecake is firm around the edges but the center (about the size of a quarter) is still jiggly.

Remove the roasting pan from the oven, and then remove the cheesecake from the water bath and the foil from the sides of the springform pan. Gently run a small sharp knife or spatula around the edges of the pan.

Allow to cool at room temperature, then refrigerate for at least 8 hours to set completely. Gently run a small sharp knife or spatula around the edges of the pan, release the latch on the pan, and lift the ring straight up. Refrigerate until ready to serve.

To garnish: When ready to serve, plate each slice individually and garnish with fresh fruit or sauce.

Yield: One 10-inch (25 cm) cheesecake

Serving Suggestions

This cheesecake is beautiful and delicious on its own, but for a pop of color serve with fresh seasonal fruit or a fruit sauce, such as blueberry or strawberry (page 146).

Variation: Manhattan Cocktail Cheesecake

Prepare the Flaky Dough Crust as directed on page 21. For the batter, omit the vanilla extract and add 2 tablespoons (30 ml) bourbon, 1 tablespoon (15 ml) sweet vermouth, and 1 tablespoon (6 g) finely grated orange zest. Garnish each slice with a maraschino cherry.

Philadelphia-Style Cheesecake

This basic cheesecake can easily be made with all cream cheese or all Neufchâtel for an even lighter version. Feel free to change the flavor by using any of your favorite extracts.

CRUST
Cookie Crust made with graham crackers
(page 17)

CHEESECAKE
1½ pounds (680 g) cream cheese

1½ pounds (680 g) Neufchâtel

2 cups (400 g) sugar

6 large eggs

1 tablespoon (15 ml) vanilla extract

GARNISH
Classic Cherry Topping (page 148)

To make the crust: Preheat the oven to 350°F (180°C, or gas mark 4). Follow the instructions on page 17 for the Cookie Crust, using graham crackers for the cookies. Let cool completely before adding the cheesecake batter.

To make the cheesecake: Preheat the oven to 325°F (170°C, or gas mark 3).

In the bowl of an electric mixer, using the paddle attachment, mix the cream cheese and Neufchâtel on low speed until softened, scraping down the sides of the bowl, underneath the paddle, and the paddle frequently with a rubber spatula, about 2 minutes. Add the sugar and continue mixing on low and scraping down the sides, bottom, and paddle until there are no visible lumps. Add the eggs, one at a time, and mix just until combined, about 10 seconds after each egg. Stir in the vanilla.

Prepare the springform pan for a water bath and place in the roasting pan (see page 30). Pour the batter over the crust and level it with a small offset spatula. Place in the oven and pour almost boiling water into the roasting pan (it should come up halfway around the sides of the pan). Bake for about 1 hour, until the cheesecake is firm around the edges, but still jiggly in the center (the jiggly part should be about the size of a quarter).

Remove from the oven and remove the cheesecake from the water bath. Remove the foil from the sides of the pan. Gently run a small sharp knife or small spatula around the edges of the pan to loosen the cheesecake from the sides. Allow to cool at room temperature. Place in the refrigerator for at least 8 hours (this will help the cheesecake set completely).

To unmold the cheesecake, gently run a small sharp knife or small spatula around the edges of the pan. Release the latch on the side of the pan and then lift the ring straight up. Refrigerate until ready to serve.

To garnish: When ready to serve, plate each slice individually and pour 2 tablespoons (30 g) of the cherry topping on the plate.

Yield: One 10-inch (25 cm) cheesecake

Variation: Maple Macadamia Cheesecake

Follow the instructions on page 17 to make a macadamia nut crust. For the batter, reduce the sugar to 1 cup (200 g) and add ⅓ cup (80 ml) maple syrup. Serve with Macadamia Nut Brittle.

Chicago-Style Cheesecake

If you want a true Chicago-style cheesecake, this is it—firm, yet still light. For a less smooth texture, the cream cheese can be replaced with all ricotta or even half cream cheese and half ricotta. This cheesecake is also delicious using your favorite liqueur, but no more than ¼ cup (60 ml) in the recipe

CRUST

Flaky Dough Crust, Sweet Dough Crust, or
   Nut Crust (page 21, 22, or 17)

CHEESECAKE

2½ (1135 g) pounds cream cheese

1½ cups (300 g) sugar

3 tablespoons (24 g) all-purpose flour

4 large eggs

4 large egg yolks

½ cup (120 ml) heavy cream

1 tablespoon (15 ml) vanilla extract

1 tablespoon (6 g) lemon zest (optional)

To make the crust: Preheat the oven to 350ºF (180ºC, or gas mark 4). Follow the instructions on page 21, 22, or 17 for the Flaky Dough Crust, Sweet Dough Crust, or Nut Crust. Let cool completely before adding the cheesecake batter.

To make the cheesecake: Preheat the oven to 325ºF (170ºC, or gas mark 3).

In the bowl of an electric mixer, using the paddle attachment, mix the cream cheese on low speed until softened, scraping down the sides of the bowl, underneath the paddle, and the paddle frequently with a rubber spatula, about 2 minutes. Add the sugar and flour and continue mixing on low and scraping down the sides, bottom, and paddle until there are no visible lumps. Add the eggs, one at a time, and mix just until combined, about 10 seconds after each egg. Add the yolks, two at a time, and mix just until combined, about 10 seconds after each addition. Stir in the heavy cream, vanilla, and lemon zest.

Prepare the springform pan for a water bath (see page 30). Place the springform pan in a large cake pan or a roasting pan (one that is around the same height or lower than your springform pan). Pour the batter over the crust and level it with a small offset spatula. Place in the oven and pour almost boiling water into the roasting pan (it should come up halfway around the sides of the pan). Bake for about 1 hour, until the cheesecake is firm around the edges, but still jiggly in the center (the jiggly part should be about the size of a quarter).

Remove from the oven and remove the cheesecake from the water bath. Remove the foil from the sides of the pan. Gently run a small sharp knife or small spatula around the edges of the pan to loosen the cheesecake from the sides. Allow to cool at room temperature. Place in the refrigerator for at least 8 hours (this will help the cheesecake set completely).

To unmold the cheesecake, gently run a small sharp knife or small spatula around the edges of the pan. Release the latch on the side of the pan and then lift the ring straight up. Refrigerate until ready to serve.

Yield: One 10-inch (25 cm) cheesecake

Ricotta and Honey Cheesecake

This classic Italian cheesecake using all ricotta gives it its crumbly texture and is a perfect ending to a meal. It is not overly sweet, so raisins could be added to the batter to make it even more of a classic. There is no crust for this recipe, but you could use the Sweet Dough Crust (page 22).

CHEESECAKE

3 pounds (1.4 kg) ricotta

¼ cup (30 g) all-purpose flour

¾ cup (255 g) honey

6 large eggs

1 teaspoon orange zest

GARNISH

Sautéed Figs (page 148)

Fruit Sauce made with raspberries (page 146)

To make the cheesecake: Preheat the oven to 325°F (170°C, or gas mark 3).

In the bowl of an electric mixer, using the paddle attachment, mix the ricotta and flour on low speed until softened, scraping down the sides of the bowl, underneath the paddle, and the paddle frequently with a rubber spatula, about 2 minutes. Add the honey and continue mixing on low and scraping down the sides, bottom, and paddle until there are no visible lumps. Add the eggs, one at a time, and mix just until combined, about 10 seconds after each egg. Stir in the orange zest.

Prepare the springform pan for a water bath (see page 30). Place the springform pan in a large cake pan or a roasting pan (one that is around the same height or lower than your springform pan). Pour the batter over the crust and level it with a small offset spatula. Place in the oven and pour almost boiling water into the roasting pan (it should come up halfway around the sides of the pan). Bake for about 1 hour, until the cheesecake is firm around the edges, but still jiggly in the center (the jiggly part should be about the size of a quarter).

Remove from oven and remove the cheesecake from the water bath. Remove the foil from the sides of the pan. Gently run a small sharp knife or small spatula around the edges of the pan to loosen the cheesecake from the sides. Allow to cool at room temperature. Place in the refrigerator for at least 8 hours (this will help the cheesecake set completely).

To unmold the cheesecake, gently run a small sharp knife or small spatula around the edges of the pan. Release the latch on the side of the pan and then lift the ring straight up. Refrigerate until ready to serve.

To garnish: When ready to serve, plate each slice individually and place sautéed fig halves next to the cheesecake and 1 to 2 tablespoons (20 to 40 g) of raspberry sauce.

Yield: One 10-inch (25 cm) cheesecake

Variation: Candied Citrus Cheesecake

Stir in ½ cup (120 g) chopped candied fruits when adding the orange zest.

Japanese Soufflé Cheesecake

This is very different from the classic creamy, rich cheesecake. The texture is very light and airy, similar to a sponge cake, but with much more flavor because of the cream cheese. The flavor can be changed by omitting the citrus and using any fruit juice. For this recipe, make sure the eggs are at room temperature.

1 tablespoon (14 g) unsalted butter, melted, for pan

¾ cup (90 g) cake flour

½ cup (60 g) cornstarch

6 ounces (168 g) cream cheese, cut into 1-inch (2.5 cm) pieces

½ cup (112 g) unsalted butter, cut into 1-inch (2.5 cm) pieces

½ cup (120 ml) milk

8 large eggs, separated, at room temperature

2 tablespoons (30 ml) lemon juice

1 teaspoon lemon zest

1 teaspoon orange zest

Pinch of salt

½ cup (100 g) sugar

Preheat the oven to 375°F (190°C, or gas mark 5). Brush the melted butter on the bottom and sides of the springform pan; set aside.

In a medium-size bowl, sift together the cake flour and cornstarch; set aside.

In another medium-size bowl, combine the cream cheese, butter, and milk. Place over a double boiler, stirring occasionally, until the mixture is melted. At this point, it will look like buttermilk. Remove from the heat and set aside to cool slightly. Whisk in the egg yolks, one at a time, until completely combined. Whisk in the lemon juice, lemon zest, and orange zest. Combine with the cake flour/cornstarch mixture; set aside.

In the bowl of an electric mixer, combine the egg whites and a pinch of salt. Using a whip attachment, whisk on medium speed. Once the egg whites become very frothy and an almost soft peak, increase the speed to medium-high. In a slow, steady stream, gradually pour in the sugar. Continue whisking until the egg whites are glossy and thick, and almost to a stiff peak, being careful not to over whip (over-whipped egg whites would look grainy).

Remove the egg whites from the mixer and add one-eighth of them to the melted cream cheese mixture; whisk until completely combined. Using a large rubber spatula, add half of the remaining egg whites and begin to fold in by cutting down the center of the mixture with the wide side of the spatula, lifting the mixture up, and turning

over. Rotate the bowl 90 degrees and repeat one more time. Add the remaining egg whites and continue folding until the egg whites are just fully incorporated.

Prepare the springform pan for a water bath (see page 30). Place the springform pan in a large cake pan or a roasting pan (one that is around the same height or lower than your springform pan). Pour the batter into the prepared pan and level it with a small offset spatula. Immediately place in the oven and pour almost boiling water into the roasting pan (it should come up halfway around the sides of the pan). Bake for about 50 minutes, or until the cake springs back when touched.

Remove from the oven and remove the cheese-cake from the water bath. Remove the foil from the sides of the pan. Gently run a small sharp knife or small spatula around the edges of the pan to loosen the cheesecake from the sides. Allow to cool at room temperature.

To unmold the cheesecake, gently run a small sharp knife or small spatula around the edges of the pan. Release the latch on the side of the pan and then lift the ring straight up. The cake is best wrapped in plastic wrap and stored at room temperature.

Yield: One 10-inch (25 cm) cheesecake

Brazilian Cheesecake

This cheesecake is inspired by flan, and is rich, sweet, and creamy. If you prefer a lighter texture and a less sweet version, you can substitute yogurt for the condensed milk.

CRUST
Nut Crust or Cookie Crust made with
   graham crackers (page 17)

CHEESECAKE
2 pounds (908 g) cream cheese

¼ cup (30 g) all-purpose flour

1 can (14 ounces, or 425 ml) sweetened
   condensed milk

½ cup (120 ml) evaporated milk

¾ cup (150 g) sugar

8 large egg yolks

GARNISH
Caramel Sauce (page 151)

To make the crust: Preheat the oven to 350°F (180°C, or gas mark 4). Follow the instructions on page 17 for the Nut or Cookie Crust made with graham crackers. Let cool completely before adding the cheesecake batter.

To make the cheesecake: Preheat the oven to 325°F (170°C, or gas mark 3).

In the bowl of an electric mixer, using the paddle attachment, mix the cream cheese and flour on low speed until softened, scraping down the sides of the bowl, underneath the paddle, and the paddle frequently with a rubber spatula, about 2 minutes. While the mixer is running on low, slowly pour in the condensed milk and evaporated milk and continue mixing on low and scraping down the sides, bottom, and paddle until completely incorporated. Add the

sugar and mix just until combined. Add the egg yolks, one at a time, and mix just until combined, about 10 seconds after each yolk.

Prepare the springform pan for a water bath (see page 30). Place the springform pan in a large cake pan or a roasting pan (one that is around the same height or lower than your springform pan). Pour the batter over the crust and level it with a small offset spatula. Place in the oven and pour almost boiling water into the roasting pan (it should come up halfway around the sides of the pan). Bake for about 1 hour, until the cheesecake is firm around the edges, but still jiggly in the center (the jiggly part should be about the size of a quarter).

Remove from the oven and remove the cheesecake from the water bath. Remove the foil from the sides of the pan. Gently run a small sharp knife or small spatula around the edges of the pan to loosen the cheesecake from the sides. Allow to cool at room temperature. Place in the refrigerator for at least 8 hours (this will help the cheesecake set completely).

To unmold the cheesecake, gently run a small sharp knife or small spatula around the edges of the pan. Release the latch on the side of the pan and then lift the ring straight up. Refrigerate until ready to serve.

To garnish: When ready to serve, plate each slice individually and pour 2 to 4 tablespoons (30 to 60 g) of caramel over each slice.

Yield: One 10-inch (25 cm) cheesecake

Israeli Cheesecake

This is made with white cheese, known as "gvina levana" in Israel, but any fresh, lower fat, white soft cheese will work. The texture is very light and smooth. Although traditionally it is made with vanilla extract, your favorite extract can be used as a substitute.

CRUST

Nut Crust or Cookie Crust made with graham crackers (page 17)

CHEESECAKE

3 containers (8 ounces, or 225 g each) of 9 percent white cheese

⅔ cup (132 g) sugar

6 large eggs

2 teaspoons vanilla extract

TOPPING

1¾ cups (420 g) sour cream

⅓ cup (66 g) sugar

1 teaspoon vanilla extract

GARNISH

Pomegranate Glaze (page 148)

1 cup (128 g) pomegranate seeds (optional)

To make the crust: Preheat the oven to 350ºF (180ºC, or gas mark 4). Follow the instructions on page 17 for the Nut or Cookie Crust made with graham crackers. Let cool completely before adding the cheesecake batter.

To make the cheesecake: Preheat the oven to 325ºF (170ºC, or gas mark 3).

In the bowl of an electric mixer, using the paddle attachment, mix the cheese on low speed until softened, scraping down the sides of the bowl, underneath the paddle, and the paddle frequently with a rubber spatula, about 1 minute. Add the sugar and continue mixing on low and scraping down the sides, bottom, and paddle until combined, about 1 minute. Add the eggs, one at a time, and mix just until combined, about 10 seconds after each egg. Stir in the vanilla.

Prepare the springform pan for a water bath (see page 30). Place the springform pan in a large cake pan or a roasting pan (one that is around the same height or lower than your springform pan). Pour the batter over the crust and level it with a small offset spatula. Place in the oven and pour almost boiling water into the roasting pan (it should come up halfway around the sides of the pan). Bake for about 50 minutes, until the cheesecake is firm around the edges, but still jiggly in the center (the jiggly part should be about the size of a quarter). Remove from oven and allow to cool for 15 minutes.

To make the topping: In a medium-size bowl, whisk together the sour cream, sugar, and vanilla.

Once the cheesecake has cooled for 15 minutes, pour on the topping, return to the oven, and bake for an additional 10 minutes. Remove the cheesecake from the oven and remove the cheesecake from the water bath. Remove the foil from the sides of the pan. Gently run a small sharp knife or small spatula around the edges of the pan to loosen the cheesecake from the sides. Allow to cool at room temperature. Place in the refrigerator for at least 8 hours (this will help the cheesecake set completely).

To unmold the cheesecake, gently run a small sharp knife or small spatula around the edges of the pan. Release the latch on the side of the pan, and then lift the ring straight up. Refrigerate until ready to serve.

To garnish: When ready to serve, plate each slice individually and pour 2 tablespoons (30 ml) of the glaze on the top of the cheesecake, then sprinkle with 1 tablespoon (8 g) of pomegranate seeds.

Yield: One 10-inch (25 cm) cheesecake

Variation: German Cheesecake

Substitute 26 ounces (750 g) of quark for the white cheese and 1 tablespoon (15 ml) strained lemon juice for the vanilla extract.

Modern Cheesecakes

"Fun and updated" describes these delicious and stunning, yet easy-to-make cheesecakes that are sure to be a hit.

White Chocolate Cheesecake with Cranberry Jewels

This is one of my favorites; the silky white cheesecake contrasts with the chocolate crust, and the top features crunchy, sweet, yet tart poached cranberries. For best results, the cranberries should be made the day the cake will be served.

CRUST
Any chocolate crust variation (pages 17 to 22)

CHEESECAKE
8 ounces (225 g) white chocolate, finely chopped

½ cup (120 ml) heavy cream

2 pounds (908 g) Neufchâtel cheese

2 tablespoons (15 g) flour

⅔ cup (133 g) sugar

3 large eggs

1 teaspoon vanilla extract

CRANBERRY JEWELS
2 cups (475 ml) water

2½ cups (500 g) sugar, divided

1 bag (12 ounces, or 336 g) cranberries

GARNISH
White chocolate curls or shavings (page 150)

To make the crust: Preheat the oven to 350ºF (180ºC, or gas mark 4). Follow the instructions for any chocolate crust variation (pages 17 to 22). Let cool completely before adding the cheesecake batter.

To make the cheesecake: Preheat the oven to 325ºF (170ºC, or gas mark 3).

Place the chocolate in a heatproof bowl; set aside. In a medium-size saucepan, heat the cream over medium-high heat until it just comes to a boil. Pour immediately over the chocolate and shake the bowl back and forth for 30 seconds, then allow to stand for 1 minute. Whisk until smooth; set aside.

Meanwhile, in the bowl of an electric mixer, using the paddle attachment, mix the Neufchâtel cheese and flour on low speed until softened, scraping down the sides of the bowl, underneath the paddle, and the paddle frequently with a rubber spatula, about 2 minutes. Add the sugar and continue mixing on low and scraping down the sides, bottom, and paddle until there are no visible lumps. Add the eggs, one at a time, and mix just until combined, about 10 seconds after each egg. Stir in the vanilla and white chocolate mixture.

Prepare the springform pan for a water bath (see page 30). Place the springform pan in a large cake pan or a roasting pan (one that is around the same height or lower than your springform pan). Pour the batter over the crust and level it with a small offset spatula. Place in the oven and pour almost boiling water into the roasting pan (it should come up halfway around the sides of the pan). Bake for about 1 hour, until the cheesecake is firm around the edges, but still jiggly in the center (the jiggly part should be about the size of a quarter).

Remove from the oven and remove the cheesecake from the water bath. Remove the foil from the sides of the pan. Gently run a small sharp knife or small spatula around the edges of the pan to loosen the cheesecake from the sides. Allow to cool at room temperature. Place in the refrigerator for at least 8 hours (this will help the cheesecake set completely).

To unmold the cheesecake, gently run a small sharp knife or small spatula around the edges of the pan. Release the latch on the side of the pan and then lift the ring straight up.

To make the cranberry jewels: Combine the water and 2 cups (400 g) of the sugar in a medium-size saucepan and bring to a boil. Lower the heat and cook for another 5 minutes. Remove from the heat and add the cranberries; stir gently to coat. Allow the cranberries to sit in the syrup for 10 minutes. Meanwhile, place the remaining ½ cup (100 g) sugar on a cookie tray. Strain the cranberries completely and place half of the cranberries on the cookie tray. Roll back and forth to completely coat with sugar. Place the other half of the cranberries on a plate. Allow to rest for 30 minutes.

To garnish: Place the chocolate shavings around a 2-inch (5 cm) border on top of the cheesecake. Fill in the center with a mixture of the sugar-coated and plain cranberries. Refrigerate until ready to serve.

Yield: One 10-inch (25 cm) cheesecake

Lemon Swirl Cheesecake

This family favorite tastes exactly like lemon meringue pie, but better. The lemon curd is swirled in the batter, but it can also be left as a layer in the center if you prefer. If fromage blanc is not available, Greek yogurt can be substituted. Make the Swiss Meringue just before serving.

CRUST
Cookie Crust made with gingersnaps (page 17)

LEMON CURD
½ cup (120 ml) lemon juice

½ cup (100 g) sugar

4 large egg yolks

4 tablespoons (56 g) unsalted butter, cut into ½-inch (1.3 cm) pieces

CHEESECAKE
2 pounds (908 g) cream cheese

1¼ cups (250 g) sugar

1 pound (454 g) fromage blanc

5 large eggs

1 tablespoon (15 ml) lemon juice

1 cup (240 g) lemon curd, divided

SWISS MERINGUE
2 large egg whites

½ cup (100 g) sugar

1 tablespoon (15 ml) lemon juice

To make the crust: Preheat the oven to 350ºF (180ºC, or gas mark 4). Follow the instructions on page 17 for the Cookie Crust made with ginger-snaps. Let cool completely before adding the cheesecake batter.

To make the lemon curd: In a 2-quart (2 L) saucepan, whisk together the lemon juice, sugar, and egg yolks. Add the butter. Place over medium heat, whisking constantly. Once the butter begins melting, the mixture will look curdled until all the butter completely melts; whisk for about 10 minutes, until the mixture thickens slightly. Do not let the curd boil, as it will curdle. Once the mixture has thickened, remove from the heat and transfer to a bowl. Cover completely with plastic wrap and make sure the plastic wrap touches the surface of the curd directly. Place in a larger bowl filled with ice and water to cool down quickly. Refrigerate until ready to use. Can be stored in the refrigerator for up to 1 week.

To make the cheesecake: Preheat the oven to 325ºF (170ºC, or gas mark 3).

In the bowl of an electric mixer, using the paddle attachment, mix the cream cheese on low speed until softened, scraping down the sides of the bowl, underneath the paddle, and the paddle frequently with a rubber spatula, about 2 minutes. Add the sugar and continue mixing on low and scraping down the sides, bottom, and paddle until there are no visible lumps. Add the fromage blanc and mix just until combined. Add the eggs, one at a time, and mix just until combined, about 10 seconds after each egg. Stir in the lemon juice and ½ cup (120 g) of the lemon curd.

Pour the batter over the crust and spread with a small offset spatula to level it. Place dollops of the remaining ½ cup (120 g) lemon curd on top of the batter. Using a knife or a small spatula, begin swirling the curd into the cheesecake batter, making either the letter *C* or *L* motion in the batter, being careful not to touch the crust.

Prepare the springform pan for a water bath (see page 30). Place the springform pan in a large cake pan or a roasting pan (one that is around the same height or lower than your springform pan). Place in the oven and pour almost boiling water into the roasting pan (it should come up halfway around the sides of the pan). Bake for about 1 hour 15 minutes, until the cheesecake is firm around the edges, but still jiggly in the center (the jiggly part should be about the size of a quarter).

Remove from the oven and remove the cheesecake from the water bath. Remove the foil from the sides of the pan. Gently run a small sharp knife or small spatula around the edges of the pan to loosen the cheesecake from the sides. Allow to cool at room temperature. Place in the refrigerator for at least 8 hours (this will help the cheesecake set completely).

To unmold the cheesecake, gently run a small sharp knife or small spatula around the edges of the pan. Release the latch on the side of the pan and then lift the ring straight up.

To make the Swiss meringue: Whisk together the egg whites and sugar in the bowl of an electric mixer. Set aside.

Fill a medium-size saucepan with 1 inch (2.5 cm) of water and place over high heat to bring to a boil; turn the heat to low. Place the bowl of egg whites and sugar on top of the saucepan, making sure the bowl does not touch the water, and whisk constantly but gently until the mixture is hot to the touch and no longer grainy, about 6 to 7 minutes.

Remove from the heat and, with the whip attachment of an electric mixer, mix the bowl of egg whites on medium-high until the mixture is thick and glossy (it will look like marshmallow fluff), about 5 to 7 minutes. You should be able to invert the bowl and the egg white mixture will stay in place. Once it is thick, stop whisking, or the mixture will overbeat and become grainy. Stir in the lemon juice.

To garnish: When ready to serve, plate each slice individually, and place a large dollop of Swiss Meringue on each slice. If desired, use a butane torch to brown the meringue until golden.

Yield: One 10-inch (25 cm) cheesecake

Variation: Key Lime or Passion Fruit Cheesecake

In the lemon curd recipe, substitute Key lime juice or passion fruit juice for the lemon juice.

Red Velvet Cheesecake

This modern mash-up of red velvet cake and cheesecake, made with a luscious mixture of cream cheese and ricotta, offers a tasty alternative to traditional ground crusts. The contrast of the red crust with the white cheesecake is visually stunning as well.

Note: When I make this cake crust, I like to double the recipe and bake the second crust in another 10-inch (25 cm) cake pan, let it cool completely, and then cut it into pieces and process in the food processor to make cake crumbs. I decorate the sides of the baked cheesecake with about ½ cup (30 g) of the crumbs, then freeze the rest for when I want to make Cheesecake Pops (page 110).

CRUST
Red Velvet Cake Crust (page 19)

CHEESECAKE
1½ pounds (680 g) cream cheese

1½ pounds (680 g) ricotta

1 cup (200 g) sugar

¼ cup (60 ml) heavy cream

5 large eggs

1 tablespoon (15 ml) vanilla extract

GARNISH
2 pints (440 g) raspberries (optional)

To make the crust: Preheat the oven to 350ºF (180ºC, or gas mark 4). Follow the instructions on page 19 for the Red Velvet Cake Crust. Let cool completely before adding the cheesecake batter.

To make the cheesecake: Lower the oven to 325ºF (170ºC, or gas mark 3).

In the bowl of an electric mixer, using the paddle attachment, mix the cream cheese and ricotta on low speed until softened, scraping down the sides of the bowl, underneath the paddle, and the paddle frequently with a rubber spatula, about 2 minutes. Add the sugar and continue mixing on low and scraping down the sides, bottom, and paddle until there are no visible lumps. Pour in the heavy cream and mix just until combined. Add the eggs, one at a time, and mix until just combined, about 10 seconds after each egg. Stir in the vanilla.

Prepare the springform pan for a water bath (see page 30). Place the springform pan in a large cake pan or a roasting pan (one that is around the same height or lower than your springform pan). Pour the batter over the crust and level it with a small offset spatula. Place in the oven and pour almost boiling water into the roasting pan (it should come up halfway around the sides of the pan). Bake for about 1 hour 10 minutes, or until the cheesecake is firm around the edges but is still jiggly in the center (the jiggly part should be about the size of a quarter).

Remove the roasting pan from the oven, and then remove the cheesecake from the water bath and the foil from the sides of the springform pan. Gently run a small sharp knife or spatula around the edges of the pan. Allow to cool at room temperature, then refrigerate for at least 8 hours to set completely.

To unmold the cheesecake, gently run a small sharp knife or spatula around the edges of the pan, release the latch on the pan, and lift the ring straight up. Refrigerate until ready to serve.

To garnish (optional): Arrange the raspberries in a circular pattern, covering the entire surface. If you made a second crust to decorate the sides of the cake with crumbs (see note, page 54). If you're right-handed, hold the cheesecake in your left hand, and with your right hand pick up and press crumbs into the sides of the cheesecake, rotating it as you work. Refrigerate until ready to serve.

Yield: One 10-inch (25 cm) cheesecake

Variation: Carrot Cake Cheesecake

Use the Carrot Cake Crust (page 20) instead of the Red Velvet Cake Crust. Prepare and bake the cheesecake batter as directed above.

Vegan Cashew Vanilla Bean Cheesecake

No one can believe this is vegan. The nuts provide a creamy, rich texture everyone will enjoy. If you aren't vegan, any crust can be paired with this, but the Chocolate Flaky Dough Crust (page 21) works wonderfully. Brazil nuts or almonds are great substitutes for the cashews.

CRUST
Vegan Coconut Crust (page 24)

CHEESECAKE
4 cups (640 g) unsalted cashews

¾ cup (180 ml) water from soaked cashews

¾ cup (180 ml) coconut oil

¼ cup (60 g) agave nectar

1 vanilla bean, split and seeds scraped out

1 tablespoon (15 ml) vanilla extract

1 tablespoon (15 ml) lemon juice

GARNISH
Dried Fruit Compote (page 147)

To make the crust: Preheat the oven to 350ºF (180ºC, or gas mark 4). Follow the instructions on page 24 for the Vegan Coconut Crust. Let cool completely before adding the cheesecake batter.

To make the cheesecake: Place the cashews in a medium-size bowl and cover with cold water by 2 inches (5 cm). Cover with plastic wrap and allow the cashews to soak for at least 8 hours to overnight in the refrigerator. Drain the cashews, reserving ¾ cup (180 ml) of the water.

In the bowl of a food processor, add the cashews and begin to purée until very fine; it will look like chunky peanut butter. With the mixer still running, slowly add the reserved water. Stop the mixer and scrape the cashews down. Turn the processor back on and slowly add the oil, and then the agave, vanilla bean seeds, vanilla extract, and lemon juice. Remove from the processor and pour the cheesecake batter over the baked crust, using an offset spatula to smooth the top. Place in the refrigerator for at least 6 hours to firm up.

To unmold the cheesecake, gently run a small sharp knife or small spatula around the edges of the pan. Release the latch on the side of the pan and then lift the ring straight up. Refrigerate until ready to serve.

To garnish: When ready to serve, plate each slice individually and pour 2 tablespoons (30 g) of Dried Fruit Compote on the plate.

Yield: One 10-inch (25 cm) cheesecake

Saffron Cheesecake with Sautéed Pineapple

This is my favorite cheesecake in the book. It has a unique flavor that friends and family agreed was surprisingly their favorite, too. Of course, you can omit the saffron and substitute different herbs and spices.

CRUST
Nut Crust made with pistachios (page 17)

CHEESECAKE
1 cup (235 ml) heavy cream

1 teaspoon packed finely grated orange zest

½ teaspoon saffron threads (not packed)

1½ pounds (680 g) cream cheese

1 tablespoon (8 g) cornstarch

1¼ cups (250 g) sugar

2 cups (480 g) whole milk plain yogurt

4 large eggs

GARNISH
Sautéed Pineapple (page 148)

To make the crust: Preheat the oven to 350°F (180°C, or gas mark 4). Follow the instructions on page 17 for the Nut Crust, using pistachios. Let cool completely before adding the cheesecake batter.

To make the cheesecake: Lower the oven to 325°F (170°C, or gas mark 3).

In a medium-size saucepan, combine the heavy cream, zest, and saffron; bring to a boil. Turn off the heat, cover, and allow to steep for 5 minutes. Strain the mixture, discarding the saffron and zest. Set aside to cool completely.

In the bowl of an electric mixer, using the paddle attachment, mix the cream cheese and cornstarch on low speed until softened, scraping down the sides of the bowl, underneath the paddle, and the paddle frequently with a rubber spatula, about 2 minutes. Add the sugar and continue mixing on low and scraping down the sides, bottom, and paddle until there are no visible lumps. Add the yogurt and mix just until combined. Add the eggs, one at a time, and mix just until combined, about 10 seconds after each egg. Stir in the cooled heavy cream.

Prepare the springform pan for a water bath (see page 30). Place the springform pan in a large cake pan or a roasting pan (one that is around the same height or lower than your springform pan). Pour the batter over the crust and level it with a small offset spatula. Place in the oven and pour almost boiling water into the roasting pan (it should come up halfway around the sides of the pan). Bake for about 1 hour 40 minutes, until the cheesecake is firm around the edges, but still jiggly in the center (the jiggly part should be about the size of a quarter).

Remove from the oven and remove the cheesecake from the water bath. Remove the foil from the sides of the pan. Gently run a small sharp knife or small spatula around the edges of the pan to loosen the cheesecake from the sides. Allow to cool at room temperature. Place in the refrigerator for at least 8 hours (this will help the cheesecake set completely).

To unmold the cheesecake, gently run a small sharp knife or small spatula around the edges of the pan. Release the latch on the side of the pan and then lift the ring straight up. Optional: For a beautiful presentation, invert the cheesecake onto a platter so the pistachio crust is on the top.

To garnish: When ready to serve, plate each slice individually and serve with about ¼ cup (60 g) of the Sautéed Pineapple.

Yield: One 10-inch (25 cm) cheesecake

Variation: Chai Tea Cheesecake

Use a Cookie Crust (page 17). For the infused cream, use 1¼ cups (300 ml) heavy cream. Omit the orange zest and saffron and instead steep it with 1½ tablespoons (12 g) loose black tea such as Darjeeling, 6 crushed cardamom pods, 5 crushed cloves, 5 black peppercorns, 1 crushed cinnamon stick, and a 1-inch (2.5 cm) piece of peeled fresh ginger, cut into rounds.

Gluten-Free Triple Chocolate Cheesecake

This modern cheesecake is crust free! If you just cannot do without the crust, use gluten-free vanilla or chocolate wafer cookies in the basic Cookie Crust recipe (page 17).

CHEESECAKE

2 pounds (908 g) cream cheese

1¼ cups (250 g) sugar

4 large eggs

5 ounces (140 g) milk chocolate, melted

5 ounces (140 g) white chocolate, melted

GARNISH

Semisweet chocolate shavings (page 150)

Chocolate Glaze (page 150)

To make the cheesecake: Preheat the oven to 325ºF (170ºC, or gas mark 3).

In the bowl of an electric mixer, using the paddle attachment, mix the cream cheese on low speed until softened, scraping down the sides of the bowl, underneath the paddle, and the paddle frequently with a rubber spatula, about 2 minutes. Add the sugar and continue mixing on low and scraping down the sides, bottom, and paddle until there are no visible lumps. Add the eggs, one at a time, and mix just until combined, about 10 seconds after each egg.

Divide the batter in half between 2 separate bowls. Pour the melted milk chocolate all at once into one bowl and stir with a rubber spatula until completely combined. Pour the melted white chocolate all at once into the other bowl and stir with a rubber spatula until completely combined.

Prepare the springform pan for a water bath (see page 30). Place the springform pan in a large cake pan or a roasting pan (one that is around the same height or lower than your springform pan). Pour the milk chocolate batter into the pan and gently spread with an offset spatula to level it. Dollop the white chocolate batter over the milk chocolate batter and spread with an offset spatula. Place in the oven and pour almost boiling water into the roasting pan, about halfway around the sides of the pan. Bake for about 1 hour 10 minutes, until the cheesecake is firm around the edges, but still jiggly in the center (the jiggly part should be about the size of a quarter).

Remove from the oven and remove the cheesecake from the water bath. Remove the foil from the sides of the pan. Gently run a sharp knife or spatula around the edges of the pan to loosen the cheesecake from the sides. Allow to cool. Place in the refrigerator for at least 8 hours (this will help the cheesecake set completely).

To unmold the cheesecake, gently run a small sharp knife or small spatula around the edges of the pan. Release the latch on the side of the pan and then lift the ring straight up.

To garnish: If you are right-handed, hold the cheesecake in your left hand (make sure the bottom of the springform pan is wiped clean) and with your right hand use a large offset spatula to pick up the chocolate shavings. Press the side of the spatula with the shavings into the side of the cheesecake. You can cover the entire side of the cake or just the bottom half. Rotate the cheesecake slightly to press in more shavings. Continue to pick up shavings with the spatula and press into the sides until you have shavings all the way around the bottom of the cheesecake. Place the cheesecake on a flat surface, pour the glaze in the middle of the cheesecake, and use an offset spatula to swirl the glaze over the top of the cheesecake. Refrigerate until ready to serve.

Yield: One 10-inch (25 cm) cheesecake

Avocado Cheesecake with Almond Brittle

Although avocado may seem unlikely in a dessert, it is a popular ingredient in many countries. Don't shy away from making this one, as it is quite delicious. This was inspired by a dessert one of my students made, which was simply avocado drizzled with honey and topped with toasted almonds.

CRUST
Nut Crust made with almonds (page 17)

CHEESECAKE
2 large ripe avocados

2 pounds (908 g) cream cheese

2 tablespoons (16 g) almond flour

½ cup (100 g) sugar

2 tablespoons (40 g) honey

3 large eggs

1 cup (240 g) yogurt

1 tablespoon (15 ml) lemon juice

GARNISH
Nut Brittle made with almonds (page 152)

To make the crust: Preheat the oven to 350°F (180°C, or gas mark 4). Follow instructions on page 17 for the Nut Crust, using almonds. Cool completely before adding the cheesecake batter.

To make the cheesecake: Lower the oven to 325°F (170°C, or gas mark 3).

Slice the avocados lengthwise around the pit. Using a spoon, scoop out the pit and discard. Scoop out the avocado from the skin. Place the avocado in a food processor and process until the avocado is completely puréed. Use within 20 minutes, or it will begin to discolor.

In the bowl of an electric mixer, using the paddle attachment, mix the cream cheese and almond flour on low speed until softened, scraping down the sides of the bowl, underneath the paddle, and the paddle frequently with a rubber spatula, about 2 minutes. Add the sugar and honey and continue mixing on low and scraping down the sides, bottom, and paddle until there are no visible lumps. Add the avocado purée and mix for another 30 seconds until combined. Add the eggs, one at a time, and mix just until combined, about 10 seconds after each egg. Add the yogurt and mix until just combined. Stir in the lemon juice.

Prepare the springform pan for a water bath (see page 30). Place the springform pan in a large cake pan or a roasting pan (one that is around the same height or lower than your springform pan). Pour the batter over the crust and level it with a small offset spatula. Place in the oven and pour almost boiling water into the roasting pan (it should come up halfway around the sides of the pan). Bake for about 1 hour, until the cheesecake is firm around the edges, but still jiggly in the center (the jiggly part should be about the size of a quarter).

Remove from the oven and remove the cheesecake from the water bath. Remove the foil from the sides of the pan. Gently run a small sharp knife or small spatula around the edges of the pan to loosen the cheesecake from the sides. Allow to cool at room temperature. Place in the refrigerator for at least 8 hours (this will help the cheesecake set completely).

To unmold the cheesecake, run a sharp knife or spatula around the edges of the pan. Release the latch on the side of the pan and then lift the ring straight up. Refrigerate until ready to serve.

To garnish: When ready to serve, plate each slice individually and garnish with a piece of brittle leaning up against the side of the cheesecake.

Yield: One 10-inch (25 cm) cheesecake

Vegan Maple Banana Cheesecake

People are surprised that this eggless cheesecake is baked, but this vegan version uses vegan cream cheese and silken tofu to give it a silky smooth texture. Paired with banana and maple, it is a perfect flavor combination. If you want to use dairy for this, substitute regular cream cheese for the vegan and sour cream for the tofu and add 4 eggs.

CRUST
Vegan Coconut Crust (page 24)

CHEESECAKE
2 large bananas

8 ounces (225 g) silken tofu

2 pounds (908 g) vegan cream cheese

¾ cup (170 g) packed brown sugar

½ cup (120 ml) maple syrup

2 teaspoons vanilla extract

1 teaspoon ground cinnamon

CARAMELIZED BANANAS
4 medium-size bananas

3 tablespoons (36 g) sugar

To make the crust: Preheat the oven to 350ºF (180ºC, or gas mark 4). Follow the instructions on page 24 for the Vegan Coconut Crust. Let cool completely before adding the cheesecake batter.

To make the cheesecake: Lower the oven to 325ºF (170ºC, or gas mark 3).

Place the bananas in a food processor and process until puréed. Measure 1 cup (225 g) of the purée and set aside. Rinse out the food processor and add the silken tofu and process until smooth and creamy. Set aside.

In the bowl of an electric mixer, using the paddle attachment, mix the cream cheese on low speed until softened, scraping down the sides of the bowl, underneath the paddle, and the paddle frequently with a rubber spatula, about 2 minutes.

Add the brown sugar and continue mixing on low and scraping down the sides, bottom, and paddle until there are no visible lumps. Add the puréed bananas and tofu; mix just until combined. Stir in the maple syrup, vanilla, and cinnamon.

Prepare the springform pan for a water bath (see page 30). Place the springform pan in a roasting pan around the same height or lower than your springform pan. Pour the batter over the crust and level it with a small offset spatula. Place in the oven and pour almost boiling water into the roasting pan (it should come up halfway around the sides of the pan). Bake for about 1 hour 15 minutes, until the cheesecake is firm around the edges, but still jiggly in the center (the jiggly part should be about the size of a quarter).

Remove from the oven and remove the cheesecake from the water bath. Remove the foil from the sides of the pan. Gently run a small sharp knife or small spatula around the edges of the pan to loosen the cheesecake from the sides. Allow to cool at room temperature. Place in the refrigerator for at least 8 hours (this will help the cheesecake set completely).

To unmold the cheesecake, run a sharp knife or spatula around the edges of the pan. Release the latch on the side of the pan and then lift the ring straight up. Refrigerate until ready to serve.

To make the bananas: Just before serving, slice each banana on a diagonal into 8 slices. Spread on a baking sheet. Sprinkle each slice with ¼ teaspoon of sugar. Using a butane torch, caramelize the sugar until golden brown. To serve, plate each slice individually and top with 2 pieces of caramelized banana.

Yield: One 10-inch (25 cm) cheesecake

Goat Cheese and Rose Cheesecake

Although this cheesecake has honey, it is not that sweet and is more akin to having a cheese for dessert. If you like it sweeter, add an extra ⅓ cup (70 g) sugar. Also, cream cheese can be substituted for the goat cheese for a creamier cheesecake.

CRUST
Nut Crust made with pistachios (page 17)

CHEESECAKE
1½ cups (355 ml) heavy cream

⅓ cup (20 g) dried rose petals

2⅔ pounds (1.2 kg) goat cheese

⅔ cup (230 g) honey

6 eggs

GARNISH
Fresh organic rose petals

Rose Syrup (page 155)

To make the crust: Preheat the oven to 350°F (180°C, or gas mark 4). Follow the instructions on page 17 for the Nut Crust, using pistachios. Let cool completely before adding the cheesecake batter.

To make the cheesecake: Lower the oven to 325°F (170°C, or gas mark 3).

In a medium-size saucepan, heat the heavy cream just until boiling. Remove from the heat and add the rose petals. Cover the pan and set aside for 15 minutes. Strain the mixture, pressing down on rose petals to extract as much of the cream as possible. Set aside to cool to room temperature.

In the bowl of an electric mixer, using the paddle attachment, mix the goat cheese on low speed until softened, scraping down the sides of the bowl, underneath the paddle, and the paddle frequently with a rubber spatula, about 2 minutes. Add the honey and continue mixing on low and scraping down the sides, bottom, and paddle until combined, about 1 minute. Add the eggs, one at a time, and mix just until combined, about 10 seconds after each egg. Slowly stir in the infused heavy cream.

Prepare the springform pan for a water bath (see page 30). Place the springform pan in a large cake pan or a roasting pan (one that is around the same height or lower than your springform pan). Pour the batter over the crust and level it with a small offset spatula. Place in the oven and pour almost boiling water into the roasting pan (it should come up halfway around the sides of the pan). Bake for about 55 minutes, until the cheesecake is firm around the edges, but still jiggly in the center (the jiggly part should be about the size of a quarter).

Remove from the oven and remove the cheesecake from the water bath. Remove the foil from the sides of the pan. Gently run a small sharp knife or small spatula around the edges of the pan to loosen the cheesecake from the sides. Allow to cool at room temperature. Place in the refrigerator for at least 8 hours (this will help the cheesecake set completely).

To unmold the cheesecake, gently run a small sharp knife or small spatula around the edges of the pan. Release the latch on the side of the pan and then lift the ring straight up. Refrigerate until ready to serve.

To garnish: Top with fresh rose petals and drizzle with Rose Syrup.

Yield: One 10-inch (25 cm) cheesecake

Variation: Goat Cheese with Honey and Lavender Cheesecake

Use a Cookie Crust (page 17) or Flaky Dough Crust (page 21) and use 1 tablespoon (2 g) dried lavender in place of the rose petals.

Seasonal Cheesecakes

This is perhaps my favorite chapter, as using ingredients in season speaks to me the most. These are best served at their appropriate time of year, but really could be made at any time.

Caramel Apple Crumb Cheesecake

This is delicious with the goat cheese, but you can use all cream cheese if you prefer or use an equal amount of mascarpone for the goat cheese. The crumb crust and topping make this taste almost like an apple pie.

CRUST
Streusel Crumb Crust (page 24)

APPLES
1 tablespoon (14 g) unsalted butter
2 Granny Smith apples, peeled and cut into
    ½-inch (1.3 cm) dice
1 teaspoon ground cinnamon

CHEESECAKE
1 pound (454 g) cream cheese
1 pound (454 g) goat cheese
½ cup (100 g) granulated sugar
4 large eggs
1 teaspoon vanilla extract
½ teaspoon ground cinnamon

GARNISH
Caramel Sauce (page 151)

To make the apples: In a large sauté pan, heat the butter over medium-high heat. Once melted, add the apples all at once and cook for 4 to 5 minutes, stirring occasionally, until the apples are just beginning to soften. Remove from the heat and stir in the cinnamon. Allow to cool completely.

To make the cheesecake: Lower the oven to 325°F (170°C, or gas mark 3).

In the bowl of an electric mixer, using the paddle attachment, mix the cream cheese and goat cheese on low speed until softened, scraping down the sides of the bowl, underneath the paddle, and the paddle frequently with a rubber spatula, about 2 minutes. Add the granulated sugar and continue mixing on low and scraping down the sides, bottom, and paddle until there are no visible lumps. Add the eggs, one at a time, and mix just until combined, about 10 seconds after each egg. Stir in the vanilla and ground cinnamon.

Prepare the springform pan for a water bath (see page 30). Place the springform pan in a large cake pan or a roasting pan (one that is around the same height or lower than your springform pan). Pour the batter over the crust and level it with a small offset spatula. Place the cooked apples on top of cheesecake batter and then sprinkle with the remaining third of the streusel. Place in the oven and pour almost boiling water into the roasting pan (it should come up halfway around the sides of the pan). Bake for about 1 hour 10 minutes, until the cheesecake is firm around the edges, but still jiggly in the center (the jiggly part should be about the size of a quarter).

Remove from the oven and remove the cheesecake from the water bath. Remove the foil from the sides of the pan. Gently run a small sharp knife or small spatula around the edges of the pan to loosen the cheesecake from the sides. Allow to cool at room temperature. Place in the refrigerator for at least 8 hours (this will help the cheesecake set completely).

To unmold the cheesecake, gently run a small sharp knife or small spatula around the edges of the pan. Release the latch on the side of the pan and then lift the ring straight up. Refrigerate until ready to serve.

To garnish: You can either drizzle the caramel over the cheesecake while it is whole and then slice it, or plate each slice individually and pour about 1 tablespoon (15 g) on top of each slice, allowing the caramel to drip off the sides.

Yield: One 10-inch (25 cm) cheesecake

Variation: Plum Cheesecake with Almond Streusel

Substitute 3 plums for the apples. For the streusel, use ¾ cup (120 g) finely chopped almonds and omit the rolled oats.

Spiced Pumpkin Cheesecake

This is the perfect holiday cheesecake, and any type of squash, sweet potato, or yam can be substituted for the pumpkin; my personal favorites are butternut squash and sweet potato. If you prefer a coarser texture, do not purée the ricotta.

CRUST

Cookie Crust made with gingersnaps (page 17), or the Sweet Dough Crust or Cream Cheese Crust (page 22)

CHEESECAKE

1½ pounds (680 g) ricotta

1 pound (454 g) cream cheese

¾ cup (170 g) packed dark brown sugar

1 can (15 ounces, or 420 g) pumpkin purée

6 large eggs

1½ teaspoons ground cinnamon

1 teaspoon vanilla extract

¼ teaspoon ground ginger

¼ teaspoon ground cloves

GARNISH

Whipped Cream (page 150)

1 teaspoon ground cinnamon

To make the crust: Preheat the oven to 350ºF (180ºC, or gas mark 4). Follow the instructions on page 17 or 22 for the Flaky Dough, Sweet Dough, or Cream Cheese Crust. Let cool completely before adding the cheesecake batter.

To make the cheesecake: Lower the oven to 325ºF (170ºC, or gas mark 3).

Place the ricotta in the bowl of a food processor and purée until smooth and creamy, about 2 minutes. Set aside.

In the bowl of an electric mixer, using the paddle attachment, mix the ricotta and cream cheese on low speed until softened, scraping down the sides of the bowl, underneath the paddle, and the paddle frequently with a rubber spatula, about 2 minutes. Add the brown sugar and continue mixing on low and scraping down the sides, bottom, and paddle until there are no visible lumps. Add the pumpkin purée and mix just until combined. Add the eggs, one at a time, and mix just until combined, about 10 seconds after each egg. Stir in the cinnamon, vanilla, ginger, and cloves.

Prepare the springform pan for a water bath (see page 30). Place the springform pan in a large cake pan or a roasting pan (one that is around the same height or lower than your springform pan). Pour the batter over the crust and level it with a small offset spatula. Place in the oven and pour almost boiling water into the roasting pan (it should come up halfway around the sides of the pan). Bake for about 1 hour 45 minutes, until the cheesecake is firm around the edges, but still jiggly in the center (the jiggly part should be about the size of a quarter).

Remove from the oven and remove the cheesecake from the water bath. Remove the foil from the sides of the pan. Gently run a small sharp knife or small spatula around the edges of the pan to loosen the cheesecake from the sides. Allow to cool at room temperature. Place in the refrigerator for at least 8 hours (this will help the cheesecake set completely).

To unmold the cheesecake, gently run a small sharp knife or small spatula around the edges of the pan. Release the latch on the side of the pan and then lift the ring straight up. Refrigerate until ready to serve.

To garnish: When ready to serve, plate each slice individually and top with a dollop of whipped cream and a dusting of ground cinnamon.

Yield: One 10-inch (25 cm) cheesecake

Variation: Chestnut Cheesecake

Use the Cookie Crust made with gingersnaps or the Cream Cheese Crust (page 17 or 22). Omit the spices and omit the pumpkin purée. Add 1 can (15 ounces, or 420 g) chestnut purée, 2 tablespoons (30 ml) dark rum, and ½ teaspoon ground cinnamon.

Pecan Praline Cheesecake

Decadent is the only word to describe this. The bourbon pairs perfectly with the praline, but it can be left out if you prefer. If praline paste is not available, Nutella is a wonderful substitute. The hazelnut flour can also be substituted with another nut flour.

CRUST
Nut Crust made with pecans (page 17)

CHEESECAKE
2 pounds (908 g) cream cheese

1 cup (225 g) packed light brown sugar

2 tablespoons (16 g) hazelnut flour

5 large eggs

1 cup (240 g) praline paste

1 cup (240 ml) heavy cream

2 tablespoons (30 ml) bourbon

GARNISH
1 cup (160 g) coarsely ground pecans

1 cup (100 g) pecan halves

To make the crust: Preheat the oven to 350ºF (180ºC, or gas mark 4). Follow the instructions on page 17 for the Nut Crust, using pecans. Let cool completely before adding the cheesecake batter.

To make the cheesecake: Lower the oven to 325ºF (170ºC, or gas mark 3).

In the bowl of an electric mixer, using the paddle attachment, mix the cream cheese on low speed until softened, scraping down the sides of the bowl, underneath the paddle, and the paddle frequently with a rubber spatula, about 2 minutes. Add the brown sugar and hazelnut flour; continue mixing on low and scraping down the sides, bottom, and paddle until there are no visible lumps. Add the eggs, one at a time, and mix just until combined, about 10 seconds after each egg. Stir in the praline paste, heavy cream, and bourbon.

Prepare the springform pan for a water bath (see page 30). Place the springform pan in a large cake pan or a roasting pan (one that is around the same height or lower than your springform pan). Pour the batter over the crust and level it with a small offset spatula. Place in the oven and pour almost boiling water into the roasting pan (it should come up halfway around the sides of the

pan). Bake for about 1 hour 30 minutes, until the cheesecake is firm around the edges, but still jiggly in the center (the jiggly part should be about the size of a quarter).

Remove from the oven and remove the cheesecake from the water bath. Remove the foil from the sides of the pan. Gently run a small sharp knife or small spatula around the edges of the pan to loosen the cheesecake from the sides. Allow to cool at room temperature. Place in the refrigerator for at least 8 hours (this will help the cheesecake set completely).

To unmold the cheesecake, gently run a small sharp knife or small spatula around the edges of the pan. Release the latch on the side of the pan and then lift the ring straight up.

To garnish: Decorate the sides of the cheesecake by pressing the ground nuts around the sides and then place the pecan halves around the top edge. Refrigerate until ready to serve.

Yield: One 10-inch (25 cm) cheesecake

Variation: Eggnog Cheesecake

Use a graham cracker or cookie crust (page 17). Omit the brown sugar and use 1 cup (200 g) granulated sugar. Omit the hazelnut flour and use 2 tablespoons (16 g) all-purpose flour. Omit the heavy cream and praline paste and use 1½ cups (360 ml) eggnog. Add 1 teaspoon ground cinnamon and ½ teaspoon ground nutmeg when you add the bourbon. For garnish, whip 1 cup (240 ml) heavy cream with ½ teaspoon ground cinnamon and ¼ teaspoon ground nutmeg to soft peaks. Dollop on the top edges of the cheesecake.

Hot Chocolate Cheesecake

If you are craving a cup of hot chocolate, then this cheesecake is for you. This is ideal on a snowy day to satisfy anyone. The chocolate pudding can also be made with semisweet, milk, or even white chocolate.

CRUST
Any chocolate crust variation (pages 17 to 22)

CHOCOLATE PUDDING (makes 3 cups [720 g])
¼ cup (50 g) sugar

2 tablespoons (16 g) cornstarch

2 tablespoons (16 g) cocoa powder

2 large eggs

2½ cups (600 ml) milk

3 ounces (84 g) bittersweet chocolate, finely chopped

1 teaspoon vanilla extract

CHEESECAKE
1½ pounds (680 g) cream cheese

½ cup (100 g) sugar

3 tablespoons (24 g) cocoa powder, sifted

3 large eggs

GARNISH
¼ cup (60 ml) Chocolate Sauce (page 150)

1 cup (50 g) mini marshmallows

½ teaspoon ground cinnamon

To make the crust: Preheat the oven to 350ºF (180ºC, or gas mark 4). Follow the instructions (pages 17 to 22) to make any of the chocolate crust variations. Let cool completely before adding the cheesecake batter.

To make the chocolate pudding: In a medium-size saucepan, whisk together the sugar, cornstarch, and cocoa powder; whisk in the eggs and then the milk. Place over medium-high heat, whisking constantly, and bring to a boil. Once the mixture boils, continue cooking for another minute. Remove from the heat and add the chocolate and vanilla extract; whisk until smooth. Pour into a heatproof bowl and cover the pudding directly with plastic wrap. Place over a bowl of ice water to cool completely.

To make the cheesecake: Lower the oven to 325°F (170°C, or gas mark 3).

In the bowl of an electric mixer, using the paddle attachment, mix the cream cheese on low speed until softened, scraping down the sides of the bowl, underneath the paddle, and the paddle frequently with a rubber spatula, about 2 minutes. Whisk together the sugar and cocoa powder in a small bowl, add to the mixture, and continue mixing on low, scraping down the sides, bottom, and paddle until there are no visible lumps. Add the chocolate pudding and mix just until combined. Add the eggs, one at a time, and mix just until combined, about 10 seconds after each egg.

Prepare the springform pan for a water bath (see page 30). Place the springform pan in a large cake pan or a roasting pan (one that is around the same height or lower than your springform pan).

Pour the batter over the crust and level it with a small offset spatula. Place in the oven and pour almost boiling water into the roasting pan (it should come up halfway around the sides of the pan). Bake for about 1 hour 20 minutes, until the cheesecake is firm around the edges, but still jiggly in the center (the jiggly part should be about the size of a quarter).

Remove from the oven and remove the cheesecake from the water bath. Remove the foil from the sides of the pan. Gently run a sharp knife or spatula around the edges of the pan to loosen the cheesecake from the sides. Allow to cool at room temperature. Place in the refrigerator for at least 8 hours to set completely.

To unmold the cheesecake, gently run a small sharp knife or small spatula around the edges of the pan. Release the latch on the side of the pan and then lift the ring straight up.

To garnish: Pour the Chocolate Sauce on top of the cheesecake. Using a small offset spatula, spread the sauce over the top, leaving a 2-inch (5 cm) border. Top with mini marshmallows, and dust with the ground cinnamon.

Yield: One 10-inch (25 cm) cheesecake

Variation: Butterscotch Cheesecake

Use the Brown Sugar Cookie Crust (page 17). Omit the cocoa powder and bittersweet chocolate. Omit the granulated sugar and use ¾ cup (180 g) dark brown sugar. Increase the cornstarch to 3 tablespoons (24 g).

Brown Sugar Peach Cheesecake

This is the perfect summertime dessert, and the buttermilk pairs refreshingly with the peach. If buttermilk isn't available, heavy cream can be substituted. Apricot or mango will also work beautifully in this recipe.

CRUST

Cookie Crust made with graham crackers (page 17)

CHEESECAKE

3 pounds (1.4 kg) ricotta

2 tablespoons (16 g) flour

1 cup (225 g) packed brown sugar

1 cup (235 ml) buttermilk

1 cup (320g) peach purée (page 147)

5 large eggs

½ teaspoon ground cinnamon

1 tablespoon (15 ml) peach brandy (optional)

PEACH TOPPING

4 tablespoons (56 g) unsalted butter, cut into ½-inch (1.3 cm) thick pieces

¼ cup (50 g) granulated or light brown sugar

4 ripe peaches, pitted, halved, and cut into ¼-inch (6 mm) slices

1 tablespoon (15 ml) peach brandy (optional)

To make the crust: Preheat the oven to 350ºF (180ºC, or gas mark 4). Follow the instructions on page 17 for the Cookie Crust, using graham crackers. Let cool completely before adding the cheesecake batter.

To make the cheesecake: Lower the oven to 325ºF (170ºC, or gas mark 3).

In the bowl of an electric mixer, using the paddle attachment, mix the ricotta and flour on low speed until softened, scraping down the sides of the bowl, underneath the paddle, and the paddle frequently with a rubber spatula, about 2 minutes. Add the brown sugar and continue mixing on low and scraping down the sides, bottom, and paddle until there are no visible lumps. Add the buttermilk and mix just until combined. Add the peach purée and mix just until combined. Add the eggs, one at a time, and mix just until combined, about 10 seconds after each egg. Stir in the cinnamon and peach brandy, if using.

Prepare the springform pan for a water bath (see page 30). Place the springform pan in a large cake pan or a roasting pan (one that is around the same height or lower than your springform pan). Pour the batter over the crust and level it with a small offset spatula. Place in the oven and pour almost boiling water into the roasting pan (it should come up halfway around the sides of the pan). Bake for about 1 hour 15 minutes, until the

cheesecake is firm around the edges, but still jiggly in the center (the jiggly part should be about the size of a quarter).

Remove from the oven and remove the cheesecake from the water bath. Remove the foil from the sides of the pan. Gently run a small sharp knife or small spatula around the edges of the pan to loosen the cheesecake from the sides. Allow to cool at room temperature. Place in the refrigerator for at least 8 hours (this will help the cheesecake set completely).

To make the peach topping: In a large sauté pan, heat the butter and sugar over medium heat until the butter is melted and the sugar is beginning to dissolve. Add the peaches and toss to coat with the butter/sugar mixture. Cook for 3 to 5 minutes, depending on the ripeness of the peaches, until slightly softened. Remove from the heat and add the brandy, if using, stirring to combine.

To unmold the cheesecake, gently run a small sharp knife or small spatula around the edges of the pan. Release the latch on the side of the pan and then lift the ring straight up.

To garnish: When ready to serve, plate each slice individually and spoon about 4 slices of sautéed peaches on the top or side of the cheesecake.

Yield: One 10-inch (25 cm) cheesecake

Variation: Blackberry Cheesecake

Substitute 1 cup (240 g) blackberry purée (page 147) for the peach purée and 2 pints (300 g) blackberries for the peaches in the sautéed topping. Cook the blackberries for 1 to 2 minutes, or until just heated through.

Strawberry Lemonade Cheesecake

Ripe strawberries combine perfectly with lemon to make this refreshing treat. If you prefer a smoother texture for the cheesecake, purée the ricotta in a food processor before mixing with the cream cheese.

CRUST
Cookie Crust made with graham crackers (page 17)

CHEESECAKE
1 pound (454 g) cream cheese

1 pound (454 g) ricotta

1 pound (454 g) mascarpone

2 tablespoons (16 g) cornstarch

2 cups (400 g) sugar

5 large eggs

½ cup plus 2 tablespoons (150 ml) lemon juice, divided

3 tablespoons (18 g) lemon zest, divided

½ cup (85 g) crushed strawberries

STRAWBERRY-LEMON TOPPING
1 large lemon, halved lengthwise, seeded, and thinly sliced

¼ cup (50 g) sugar

2 tablespoons (30 ml) water

½ cup (85 g) quartered or sliced strawberries

To make the crust: Preheat the oven to 350ºF (180ºC, or gas mark 4). Follow the instructions on page 17 for the Cookie Crust, using graham crackers. Let cool completely before adding the cheesecake batter.

To make the cheesecake: Lower the oven to 325ºF (170ºC, or gas mark 3).

In the bowl of an electric mixer, using the paddle attachment, mix the cream cheese, ricotta, mascarpone, and cornstarch on low speed until softened, scraping down the sides of the bowl, underneath the paddle, and the paddle frequently with a rubber spatula, about 2 minutes. Add the sugar and continue mixing on low and scraping down the sides, bottom, and paddle until there are no visible lumps. Add the eggs, one at a time, and mix just until combined, about 10 seconds after each egg.

Divide the batter in half, approximately 4 cups (960 g) each in 2 bowls. To the first bowl, stir in ½ cup (120 ml) of the lemon juice and 2 tablespoons (12 g) of the lemon zest; set aside. To the second bowl, stir in the crushed strawberries, remaining 2 tablespoons (30 ml) lemon juice, and remaining 1 tablespoon (6 g) lemon zest. Set aside.

Prepare the springform pan for a water bath (see page 30). Place the springform pan in a large cake pan or a roasting pan (one that is around the same height or lower than your springform pan). Pour the strawberry batter over the crust and level it with a small offset spatula, then top with the lemon batter. Place in the oven and pour almost boiling water into the roasting pan (it should come up halfway around the sides of the pan). Bake for about 1 hour 30 minutes, until the cheesecake is firm around the edges, but still jiggly in the center (the jiggly part should be about the size of a quarter).

Remove from the oven and remove the cheesecake from the water bath. Remove the foil from the sides of the pan. Gently run a small sharp knife or small spatula around the edges of the pan to loosen the cheesecake from the sides. Allow to cool at room temperature. Place in the refrigerator for at least 8 hours (this will help the cheesecake set completely).

To unmold the cheesecake, gently run a small sharp knife or small spatula around the edges of the pan. Release the latch on the side of the pan and then lift the ring straight up. Refrigerate until ready to serve.

To make the topping: Combine the lemon slices, sugar, and water in a medium-size saucepan; bring to a boil. Reduce the heat to a simmer and cook for 7 to 8 minutes, until the lemons are softened and limp. Remove from the heat; allow to cool completely. Add the strawberries, stir to combine, and place in the center of the cake just before serving.

Yield: One 10-inch (25 cm) cheesecake

Mascarpone and Raspberry Cheesecake

1½ cups (360 g) raspberry purée
(page 147), divided

1 tablespoon (15 ml) lemon juice

1 tablespoon (15 ml) raspberry liqueur

TOPPING

1¼ cups (300 g) raspberry purée (page 147),
divided

2 teaspoons granulated gelatin

GARNISH

1 cup (25 g) freeze-dried raspberries, finely
ground in a food processor

To make the crust: Preheat the oven to 350ºF
(180ºC, or gas mark 4). Follow the instructions
on page 17 for the Cookie Crust, using graham
crackers. Let cool completely before adding the
cheesecake batter.

To make the cheesecake: Lower the oven to
325ºF (170ºC, or gas mark 3).

In the bowl of an electric mixer, using the paddle
attachment, mix the cream cheese, mascarpone,
and cornstarch on low speed until softened, scraping down the sides of the bowl, underneath the
paddle, and the paddle frequently with a rubber
spatula, about 2 minutes. Add the sugar and
continue mixing on low and scraping down the
sides, bottom, and paddle until there are no visible
lumps. Add 4 of the eggs, one at a time, and mix
just until combined, about 10 seconds after each
egg. Stir in 1 cup (240 g) of the raspberry purée,
the lemon juice, and the framboise.

Remove 2½ cups (600 g) of batter from the bowl
and place in another bowl. Whisk in the remaining egg and the remaining ½ cup (120 g)
raspberry purée.

**The raspberry purée in this recipe can be
store-bought or homemade. You can also
substitute other fruit purée.**

CRUST
Cookie Crust made with graham crackers
(page 17)

CHEESECAKE
1½ pounds (680 g) cream cheese

1 pound (454 g) mascarpone

2 tablespoons (16 g) cornstarch

¾ cup (150 g) sugar

5 large eggs, divided

Layer the batter by placing half of the first batter in the crust, then smooth the surface with a small offset spatula. Place the second batter on top, and smooth with an offset spatula. Top with remaining first batter, smoothing the top.

Prepare the springform pan for a water bath (see page 30). Place the springform pan in a large cake pan or a roasting pan (one that is around the same height or lower than your springform pan). Place in the oven and pour almost boiling water into the roasting pan (it should come up halfway around the sides of the pan). Bake for about 1 hour 30 minutes, until the cheesecake is firm around the edges, but still jiggly in the center (the jiggly part should be about the size of a quarter).

Remove from the oven and remove the cheesecake from the water bath. Remove the foil from the sides of the pan. Gently run a small sharp knife or small spatula around the edges of the pan to loosen the cheesecake from the sides. Allow to cool at room temperature. Place in the refrigerator for at least 8 hours (this will help the cheesecake set completely).

To unmold the cheesecake, gently run a small sharp knife or small spatula around the edges of the pan. Release the latch on the side of the pan and then lift the ring straight up. Refrigerate until ready to serve.

To make the topping: Make this just before you are ready to pour it on top of the cheesecake and once the cheesecake is cool. Place ¼ cup (60 g) of the raspberry purée in a small bowl. Sprinkle with the gelatin, making sure the gelatin is completely immersed and not clumped together, and allow to stand for 2 to 3 minutes. Meanwhile, in a small saucepan, heat ½ cup (120 g) of the raspberry purée over medium heat until hot, about 2 minutes. Pour over the gelatin mixture and stir until smooth and all the grains of gelatin have dissolved. Whisk in the remaining ½ cup (120 g) purée. Slowly pour the purée mixture on top of the cheesecake, making sure to get the purée all the way to the edges of the cheesecake. If the mixture is not level, use a small offset spatula to spread evenly. Place in the refrigerator and allow to set, a minimum of 4 hours.

To garnish: When ready to serve, plate each slice individually and sprinkle the plate with about 1½ teaspoons of the freeze-dried raspberries.

Yield: One 10-inch (25 cm) cheesecake

Variation: Strawberry Rhubarb Cheesecake

Use the Cream Cheese Crust (page 22). For the purée, use 3 cups (510 g) sliced strawberries, 3 cups (360 g) diced rhubarb, and ¼ cup (60 ml) water. Combine all the ingredients in a saucepan and cook over medium heat until the rhubarb is completely softened and is easily pierced with a knife. Remove from the heat and allow to cool slightly. Place in a food processor and process until completely smooth. Divide the purée and use 1½ cups (360 g) for the cheesecake and 1¼ cups (300 g) for the topping.

Fennel and Apple Cheesecake

Fennel, which has a sweet anise flavor, blends outstandingly with the apple. I was motivated to make this as a way to use up all the fennel and apples I had purchased at the farmers' market. If you like a stronger fennel flavor, you can substitute 1 tablespoon (15 ml) of fennel liqueur for the vanilla extract.

CRUST

Nut Crust (page 17)

FENNEL-APPLE PURÉE

1 cup (150 g) ¼-inch (6 mm) diced fennel bulb

½ cup (75 g) ¼-inch (6 mm) peeled, diced Granny Smith apple

½ cup (120 ml) orange juice

CHEESECAKE

2½ pounds (1 kg) ricotta

1¼ cups (250 g) granulated sugar

¼ cup (56 g) light brown sugar

5 large eggs

1 teaspoon vanilla extract

GARNISH

Apple Cider Reduction (page 149, optional)

Nut Brittle made with fennel seeds (page 152)

To make the crust: Preheat the oven to 350ºF (180ºC, or gas mark 4). Follow the instructions on page 17 for the Nut Crust. Let cool completely before adding the cheesecake batter.

To make the fennel-apple purée: Combine the fennel, apple, and orange juice in a small saucepan; bring to a boil, reduce to a simmer, cover, and cook for 5 to 7 minutes, or until very tender. Remove from the heat and cool slightly. Place the mixture in a food processor and process until completely puréed. Set aside.

To make the cheesecake: Lower the oven to 325ºF (170ºC, or gas mark 3).

In the bowl of an electric mixer, using the paddle attachment, mix the ricotta on low speed until softened, scraping down the sides of the bowl, underneath the paddle, and the paddle frequently with a rubber spatula, about 2 minutes. Add the granulated sugar and brown sugar and continue mixing on low and scraping down the sides, bottom, and paddle until there are no visible lumps. Add the cooled fennel purée and mix just until combined. Add the eggs, one at a time, and mix just until combined, about 10 seconds after each egg. Stir in the vanilla.

Prepare the springform pan for a water bath (see page 30). Place the springform pan in a large cake pan or a roasting pan (one that is around the same height or lower than your springform pan). Pour the batter over the crust and level it with a small offset spatula. Place in the oven and pour almost boiling water into the roasting pan (it should come up halfway around the sides of the pan). Bake for about 1 hour 20 minutes, until the cheesecake is firm around the edges, but still jiggly in the center (the jiggly part should be about the size of a quarter).

Remove from the oven and remove the cheesecake from the water bath. Remove the foil from the sides of the pan. Gently run a small sharp knife or small spatula around the edges of the pan to loosen the cheesecake from the sides. Allow to cool at room temperature. Place in the refrigerator for at least 8 hours (this will help the cheesecake set completely).

To unmold the cheesecake, gently run a small sharp knife or small spatula around the edges of the pan. Release the latch on the side of the pan and then lift the ring straight up. Refrigerate until ready to serve.

To garnish: Pour about 1 tablespoon (15 ml) of the Apple Cider Reduction, if using, onto each plate, top with a slice of cheesecake, and sprinkle with about 1 tablespoon (15 g) of the coarsely crushed fennel brittle.

Yield: One 10-inch (25 cm) cheesecake

Savory Cheesecakes

These cheesecakes are perfect for a first or main course.
I like to serve them with a green salad or sautéed greens.
They can also be baked in a square pan and cut into
1-inch (2.5 cm) pieces and served as hors d'oeuvres.

Blue Cheese Cheesecake with Candied Walnuts

This cheesecake is even for people who aren't blue cheese lovers. The cheese's sharp, salty tang is mellowed by the cream cheese and has a subtle flavor that is pleasing on the palate. I like to use a creamy soft cheese such as a Danish blue, but even the firmer, crumbly blues such as Gorgonzola or Roquefort work well. This is a nice change to serve as a cheese course after a meal.

CRUST

Flaky Dough, Bacon, or Parmesan and
   Herb Crust (page 21 or 23)

CHEESECAKE

1 pound (454 g) cream cheese

1 pound (454 g) blue cheese

1 cup (240 ml) heavy cream

5 large eggs

1 teaspoon dry mustard powder

½ teaspoon kosher salt

½ teaspoon ground black pepper

¼ teaspoon Tabasco

GARNISH

Candied Walnuts (page 152)

To make the crust: Preheat the oven to 350ºF (180ºC, or gas mark 4). Follow the instructions on page 21 or 23 for the Flaky Dough, Bacon, or Parmesan and Herb Crust. Let cool completely before adding the cheesecake batter.

To make the cheesecake: Lower the oven to 325ºF (170ºC, or gas mark 3).

In the bowl of an electric mixer, using the paddle attachment, mix the cream cheese and blue cheese on low speed until softened, scraping down the sides of the bowl, underneath the paddle, and the paddle frequently with a rubber spatula, about 2 minutes. Add the heavy cream in a slow stream while the mixer is running and mix just until combined. Add the eggs, one at a time, and mix just until combined, about 10 seconds after each egg. Stir in the dry mustard, salt, pepper and Tabasco.

Prepare the springform pan for a water bath (see page 30). Place the springform pan in a large cake pan or a roasting pan (one that is around the same height or lower than your springform pan). Pour the batter over the crust and level it with a small offset spatula. Place in the oven and pour almost boiling water into the roasting pan (it should come up halfway around the sides of the pan). Bake for about 1 hour, until the cheesecake is firm.

Remove from the oven and remove the cheesecake from the water bath. Remove the foil from the sides of the pan. Gently run a small sharp knife or small spatula around the edges of the pan to loosen the cheesecake from the sides. Allow to cool at room temperature. Place in the refrigerator for at least 8 hours (this will help the cheesecake set completely).

To unmold the cheesecake, gently run a small sharp knife or small spatula around the edges of the pan. Release the latch on the side of the pan and then lift the ring straight up. Refrigerate until ready to serve.

To garnish: When ready to serve, plate each slice individually and top with approximately 1 tablespoon (9 g) of candied walnuts.

Yield: One 10-inch (25 cm) cheesecake

Chive Pesto Cheesecake

I wanted to use up my abundance of chives this summer and happily decided to turn them into cheesecake. Fortunately, pesto can be made with many greens, so it is easy to change the flavor of this cheesecake. Substitute watercress, arugula, or even radish tops for the chives and for variations on the nuts, try pistachios, walnuts, or almonds. For this recipe, make sure the eggs are at room temperature.

CRUST

Bacon or Parmesan and Herb Crust
   (page 23)

CHIVE PESTO

1 cup (48 g) coarsely chopped chives

3 cloves garlic, peeled and smashed

2 tablespoons (16 g) toasted pine nuts

¼ cup (25 g) finely grated Parmesan

¼ cup (60 ml) extra-virgin olive oil

CHEESECAKE

2 pounds (908 g) ricotta

2 tablespoons (16 g) flour

4 large eggs, separated, at room temperature

¼ cup (25 g) finely grated Parmesan

1 teaspoon kosher salt

½ teaspoon ground black pepper

1 teaspoon lemon juice

GARNISH

½ cup (24 g) chopped chives, optional

½ cup (67g) toasted pine nuts, optional

To make the crust: Preheat the oven to 350ºF (180ºC, or gas mark 4). Follow the instructions on page 23 for the Bacon or Parmesan and Herb Crust. Let cool completely before adding the cheesecake batter.

To make the pesto: In the bowl of a food processor, combine the chives, garlic, and pine nuts. Process on high until almost smooth and completely combined. Stop and add the Parmesan and process just until incorporated. With the processor still running, slowly pour in the olive oil. Remove from the processor and set aside.

To make the cheesecake: Lower the oven to 325ºF (170ºC, or gas mark 3).

In the bowl of an electric mixer, using the paddle attachment, mix the ricotta and flour on low speed until softened, scraping down the sides of the bowl, underneath the paddle, and the paddle frequently with a rubber spatula, about 2 minutes. Add the pesto and mix just until combined. Add the eggs yolks, two at a time, and mix just until combined, about 10 seconds after each addition. Stir in parmesan, salt, and pepper. If you do not have a second bowl for the electric mixer, transfer this mixture to a large bowl and set aside.

In a clean bowl of an electric mixer, using the whip attachment, add the egg whites and begin mixing on medium-low until frothy. Add the lemon juice, increase the speed to high, and beat until the egg whites are thick and glossy, almost a stiff peak, about 3 to 4 minutes. Be careful not to over whip (over-whipped egg whites would look grainy at this point).

Remove the egg whites from the mixer and add one-eighth of them to the chive pesto mixture, and whisk until completely combined. Using a large rubber spatula, add half of the remaining egg whites and begin to fold in by cutting down the center of the mixture with the wide side of the spatula, lifting the mixture up, and turning over. Rotate the bowl 90 degrees and repeat one more time. Add the remaining egg whites and continue folding until the egg whites are just fully incorporated.

Prepare the springform pan for a water bath (see page 30). Place the springform pan in a large cake pan or a roasting pan (one that is around the same height or lower than your springform pan). Pour the batter over the crust and level it with a small offset spatula. Place in the oven and pour almost boiling water into the roasting pan (it should come up halfway around the sides of the pan). Bake for about 1 hour, until the cheesecake is firm around the edges, but still jiggly in the center (the jiggly part should be about the size of a quarter).

Remove from the oven and remove the cheesecake from the water bath. Remove the foil from the sides of the pan. Gently run a small sharp knife or small spatula around the edges of the pan to loosen the cheesecake from the sides. Allow to cool at room temperature. Place in the refrigerator for at least 8 hours (this will help the cheesecake set completely).

To unmold the cheesecake, gently run a small sharp knife or small spatula around the edges of the pan. Release the latch on the side of the pan and then lift the ring straight up. Refrigerate until ready to serve.

To garnish: When ready to serve, plate each slice individually and sprinkle with approximately 1½ teaspoons each of chives and pine nuts.

Yield: One 10-inch (25 cm) cheesecake

Variation: Basil Pesto Cheesecake

Omit the chives and add 1 cup (48 g) packed basil leaves.

Roasted Tomato with Parmesan Cheesecake

My son, who loves tomatoes, was the inspiration behind this cheesecake, which had sun-dried tomatoes in the batter and beefsteak tomatoes on the top, with just a hint of smokiness from the chipotle. Green Zebra tomatoes will also work for this, and look beautiful alternated with the beefsteak.

CRUST

Flaky Dough variation, Bacon, or Parmesan and Herb Crust (page 21 or 23)

CHEESECAKE

2 pounds (908 g) cream cheese

⅓ cup (37 g) minced oil-packed sun-dried tomatoes

1 tablespoon (9 g) minced chipotle pepper

5 eggs

1 teaspoon kosher salt

½ teaspoon ground black pepper

2 beefsteak tomatoes, sliced into eight ¼-inch (6 mm) slices

1 tablespoon (5 g) grated Parmesan

To make the crust: Preheat the oven to 350ºF (180ºC, or gas mark 4). Follow the instructions on page 21 or 23 for the Flaky Dough variation, Bacon, or Parmesan and Herb Crust. Let cool completely before adding the cheesecake batter.

To make the cheesecake: Lower the oven to 325ºF (170ºC, or gas mark 3).

In the bowl of an electric mixer, using the paddle attachment, mix the cream cheese on low speed until softened, scraping down the sides of the bowl, underneath the paddle, and the paddle frequently with a rubber spatula, about 2 minutes. Add the sun-dried tomatoes and chipotle pepper and mix just until combined. Add the eggs, one at a time, and mix just until combined, about 10 seconds after each egg. Stir in the salt and pepper.

Prepare the springform pan for a water bath (see page 30). Place the springform pan in a large cake pan or a roasting pan (one that is around the same height or lower than your springform pan). Pour the batter over the crust and level it with a small offset spatula. Lay the sliced tomatoes, in a circle, on top of the cheesecake. Place in the oven and pour almost boiling water into the roasting pan (it should come up halfway around the sides of the pan). Bake for about 50 minutes, until the cheesecake is firm around the edges, but still jiggly in the center (the jiggly part should be about the size of a quarter).

Remove from the oven and remove the cheesecake from the water bath. Remove the foil from the sides of the pan. Gently run a small sharp knife or small spatula around the edges of the pan to loosen the cheesecake from the sides. Allow to cool at room temperature. Place in the refrigerator for at least 8 hours (this will help the cheesecake set completely).

To unmold the cheesecake, gently run a small sharp knife or small spatula around the edges of the pan. Release the latch on the side of the pan and then lift the ring straight up. Refrigerate until ready to serve.

Before serving, sprinkle with the Parmesan cheese and place under a broiler for about 5 minutes, or until lightly golden.

Yield: One 10-inch (25 cm) cheesecake

White Bean and Herb Cheesecake

The versatility of this cheesecake is limitless. Chickpeas or black, pinto, or kidney beans will work wonderfully. Just remember the color of cheesecake will change depending on which bean you choose. Don't be tempted to leave off the Herb Oil; it enhances the flavor tremendously.

CRUST

1 tablespoon (15 ml) olive oil

½ cup (60 g) finely ground bread crumbs

(Or use any savory crust)

WHITE BEAN PURÉE

1 can (15 ounces, or 420 g) white beans

2 cloves garlic, crushed

¼ cup (60 g) tahini

¼ cup (60 ml) lemon juice

2 tablespoons (30 ml) water

½ tablespoon kosher salt

½ teaspoon ground black pepper

CHEESECAKE

2 pounds (908 g) cream cheese

4 large eggs

GARNISH

Herb Oil (page 154)

To make the crust: Pour the oil into the bottom of a 10-inch (25 cm) springform pan. Using a pastry brush, brush the oil all over the bottom and sides of the pan. Pour the bread crumbs in the bottom of the pan and rotate the pan around so that the bread crumbs cover the bottom and the sides completely. Set aside.

To make the white bean purée: In the bowl of a food processor add the white beans and garlic; process until smooth. Add the tahini, lemon juice, water, salt, and pepper and process until smooth. Remove from the bowl and set aside.

To make the cheesecake: Preheat the oven to 325°F (170°C, or gas mark 3).

In the bowl of an electric mixer, using the paddle attachment, mix the cream cheese on low speed until softened, scraping down the sides of the bowl, underneath the paddle, and the paddle frequently with a rubber spatula, about 1 minute. Add the white bean purée and mix for about 1 minute, until completely smooth. Add the eggs, one at a time, and mix just until combined, about 10 seconds after each egg.

Prepare the springform pan for a water bath (see page 30). Place the springform pan in a large cake pan or a roasting pan (one that is around the same height or lower than your springform pan). Pour the batter over the crust and level it with a small offset spatula. Place in the oven and pour almost boiling water into the roasting pan (it should come up halfway around the sides of the pan). Bake for about 1 hour, until the cheesecake is firm around the edges, but still jiggly in the center (the jiggly part should be about the size of a quarter).

Remove from the oven and remove the cheesecake from the water bath. Remove the foil from the sides of the pan. Gently run a small sharp knife or small spatula around the edges of the pan to loosen the cheesecake from the sides. Allow to cool at room temperature. Place in the refrigerator for at least 8 hours (this will help the cheesecake set completely).

To unmold the cheesecake, gently run a small sharp knife or small spatula around the edges of the pan. Release the latch on the side of the pan and then lift the ring straight up. Refrigerate until ready to serve.

To garnish: When ready to serve, plate each slice individually and pour approximately 1 tablespoon (15 ml) of the Herb Oil on top of the cheesecake.

Yield: One 10-inch (25 cm) cheesecake

Spiced Butternut Squash Cheesecake

If you want a smoother texture to this cheesecake, you can substitute cream cheese for the ricotta or purée the ricotta in a food processor. You can also use sweet potatoes, acorn squash, or pumpkin instead of the butternut squash.

CRUST
Any savory crust or Nut Crust without sugar
    (page 23 or 17)

ROASTED BUTTERNUT SQUASH PURÉE
1 pound (454 g) butternut squash

½ cup (120 ml) water

CHEESECAKE
1½ pounds (680 g) ricotta

1 pound (454 g) goat cheese

1 ounce (28 g) finely grated Parmesan cheese

1½ cups (368 g) butternut squash purée

½ cup (120 ml) heavy cream

¼ cup (60 g) tahini

5 large eggs

2 teaspoons kosher salt

1 teaspoon ground black pepper

1 teaspoon ground ginger

1 teaspoon ground cumin

½ teaspoon smoked paprika

GARNISH
Toasted Butternut Squash Seeds (page 153)

To make the crust: Preheat the oven to 350ºF (180ºC, or gas mark 4). Follow the instructions on page 23 or 17 for a savory or nut crust. Let cool completely before adding the cheesecake batter.

To make the purée: Increase the oven to 450ºF (230ºC, or gas mark 8).

Halve the squash lengthwise, scoop out the seeds, and set aside to make the Toasted Butternut Squash Seeds on page 153. Place the squash, cut-side down, in a baking pan. Pour the water into the pan. Place in the oven and bake until the squash can be pierced easily with a knife and is lightly browned, about 40 minutes. Remove from the oven and allow to cool slightly. Scoop out the flesh and mash with a fork until completely smooth or purée in a food processor. Measure out 1½ cups (368 g) and set aside.

To make the cheesecake: Lower the oven to 325ºF (170ºC, or gas mark 3).

In the bowl of an electric mixer, using the paddle attachment, mix the ricotta and goat cheese on low speed until softened, scraping down the sides of the bowl, underneath the paddle, and the paddle frequently with a rubber spatula, about 2 minutes. Add the Parmesan and mix just until incorporated, about 1 minute. Add the butternut squash purée and mix just until combined. Add the heavy cream and tahini and continue mixing until just combined. Add the eggs, one at a time, and mix just until combined, about 10 seconds after each egg. Stir in the salt, pepper, ginger, cumin, and smoked paprika.

Prepare the springform pan for a water bath (see page 30). Place the springform pan in a large cake pan or a roasting pan (one that is around the same height or lower than your springform pan).

Pour the batter over the crust and level it with a small offset spatula. Place in the oven and pour almost boiling water into the roasting pan (it should come up halfway around the sides of the pan). Bake for about 1 hour 30 minutes, until the cheesecake is firm around the edges, but still jiggly in the center (the jiggly part should be about the size of a quarter).

Remove from the oven and remove the cheesecake from the water bath. Remove the foil from the sides of the pan. Gently run a small sharp knife or small spatula around the edges of the pan to loosen the cheesecake from the sides. Allow to cool at room temperature. Place in the refrigerator for at least 8 hours (this will help the cheesecake set completely).

To unmold the cheesecake, gently run a small sharp knife or small spatula around the edges of the pan. Release the latch on the side of the pan and then lift the ring straight up. Refrigerate until ready to serve.

To garnish: When ready to serve, plate each slice individually and sprinkle with approximately 1 tablespoon (8 g) of toasted seeds.

Yield: One 10-inch (25 cm) cheesecake

Variation: Kabocha Squash Cheesecake

Use the Cornmeal Flaky Dough Crust (page 21). Instead of the butternut squash, use a kabocha squash (these are usually between 2 and 4 pounds [908 and 1816 g]). Cut off the top and bottom, cut in half, scoop out the seeds, and set aside. Place the squash, cut-side down, in a baking pan. Pour the water into the pan. Place in the oven and bake until it is easily pierced with a knife and lightly browned, about 1 hour. Remove from the oven and allow to cool slightly, and then scoop out the flesh and mash with a fork until smooth or purée in a food processor. Measure out 1½ cups (368 g) and set aside. You will have extra purée, which can be frozen for later use.

Spinach and Goat Cheese Cheesecake

This savory cheesecake and crust tastes just like spinach dip. It's great as an appetizer, and can also work as a main course when served with a salad.

CRUST
Parmesan and Herb Crust (page 23)

CHEESECAKE
1 tablespoon (14 g) grapeseed or other vegetable oil

¼ cup (40 g) minced shallot

1½ teaspoons kosher salt, divided

¾ teaspoon ground black pepper, divided

2 cups (360 g) frozen chopped spinach, thawed and drained

2 pounds (908 g) goat cheese

1½ cups (355 ml) heavy cream

5 large eggs

To make the crust: Preheat the oven top 350°F (180°C, or gas mark 4). Follow the instructions on page 23 for the Parmesan and Herb Crust. Cool completely before adding the cheesecake batter.

To make the cheesecake: Lower the oven to 325°F (170ºC, or gas mark 3).

In an 8- to 10-inch (20 to 25 cm) sauté pan, heat the grapeseed oil over medium heat. Add the shallot, season with ¼ teaspoon of the salt and ¼ teaspoon of the pepper, and cook until soft, about 3 minutes. Add the spinach and toss to combine; remove from the heat and set aside to cool.

Meanwhile, in the bowl of an electric mixer, with the paddle attachment, beat the goat cheese on low speed until softened, scraping down the sides of the bowl, underneath the paddle, and the paddle frequently with a rubber spatula, about 2 minutes. With the mixer on low, slowly pour in the heavy cream. Add the eggs, one at a time, and mix until just combined, about 10 seconds after each egg. By hand, stir in the remaining 1¼ teaspoons salt, remaining ½ teaspoon pepper, and the spinach mixture.

Prepare the springform pan for a water bath (see page 30). Place the springform pan in a large cake pan or a roasting pan (one that is around the same height or lower than your springform pan). Pour the batter over the crust and level it with a small offset spatula. Place in the oven and pour almost boiling water into the roasting pan (it should come up halfway around the sides of the pan). Bake for about 1 hour 10 minutes, or until the cheesecake is firm around the edges but is still jiggly in the center (the jiggly part should be about the size of a quarter).

Remove from the oven and remove the cheesecake from the water bath. Remove the foil from the sides of the pan. Gently run a sharp knife or spatula around the edges to loosen the cheesecake from the sides. Allow to cool at room temperature. Place in the refrigerator for at least 8 hours (this will help the cheesecake set completely).

To unmold the cheesecake, gently run a sharp knife or spatula around the edges. Release the latch on the side of the pan and then lift the ring straight up. Refrigerate until ready to serve.

Yield: One 10-inch (25 cm) cheesecake

Roasted Red Pepper and Sriracha Cheesecake

Roasted orange or yellow peppers will work equally well. You can also use farmer cheese or ricotta in place of the cottage cheese if you like a smoother texture.

CRUST
Cream Cheese Crust (page 22)

ROASTED RED PEPPER PURÉE AND SLICED PEPPER GARNISH
2 red bell peppers

CHEESECAKE
1½ pounds (680 g) cream cheese

8 ounces (227 g) cottage cheese

½ cup (90 g) roasted red pepper purée

¼ cup (60 ml) sriracha

5 large eggs

1 teaspoon kosher salt

To make the crust: Preheat the oven to 350ºF (180ºC, or gas mark 4). Follow the instructions on page 22 for the Cream Cheese Crust. Let cool completely before adding the cheesecake batter.

To make the roasted red pepper purée and garnish: Place the red peppers directly on a gas burner and rotate with tongs until blackened and charred, about 3 to 4 minutes. Remove from the heat and wrap in aluminum foil; set aside until cool, about 10 minutes. If you do not have a gas stove, preheat the oven 350ºF (180ºC, or gas mark 4), lightly coat the peppers in oil, and place on a baking tray. Place in the oven and bake until the peppers are very soft and wilted, about 1 hour. Once cool, peel the black skin off the peppers, cut off the top, and remove the core and seeds. Place one roasted pepper in a food processor and process until smooth. Measure out ½ cup (90 g) and set aside. Slice the other pepper into thin strips and set aside.

To make the cheesecake: Lower the oven to 325ºF (170ºC, or gas mark 3).

In the bowl of an electric mixer, using the paddle attachment, mix the cream cheese and cottage cheese on low speed until softened, scraping down the sides of the bowl, underneath the paddle, and the paddle frequently with a rubber spatula, about 2 minutes. Add the roasted red pepper purée and sriracha and mix just until combined. Add the eggs, one at a time, and mix just until combined, about 10 seconds after each egg. Stir in the salt and mix until combined.

Prepare the springform pan for a water bath (see page 30). Place the springform pan in a large cake pan or a roasting pan (one that is around the same height or lower than your springform pan).

Pour the batter over the crust and level it with a small offset spatula. Place in the oven and pour almost boiling water into the roasting pan (it should come up halfway around the sides of the pan). Bake for about 1 hour 10 minutes, until the cheesecake is firm around the edges, but still jiggly in the center (the jiggly part should be about the size of a quarter)

Remove from the oven and remove the cheesecake from the water bath. Remove the foil from the sides of the pan. Gently run a small sharp knife or small spatula around the edges of the pan to loosen the cheesecake from the sides. Allow to cool at room temperature. Place in the refrigerator for at least 8 hours (this will help the cheesecake set completely).

To unmold the cheesecake, gently run a small sharp knife or small spatula around the edges of the pan. Release the latch on the side of the pan and then lift the ring straight up. Refrigerate until ready to serve.

To garnish: When ready to serve, plate each slice individually and garnish with about 2 tablespoons (20 g) of the roasted red pepper strips on top.

Yield: One 10-inch (25 cm) cheesecake

Variation: Roasted Corn and Garlic Cheesecake

Use the same crust. Omit the red pepper purée and sriracha. Preheat the oven to 400ºF (200ºC, or gas mark 6). Place 2 ears of unhusked corn on a sheet tray and bake in the oven for 20 to 30 minutes, until the corn husks are golden and the corn kernels are soft. Remove from the oven and allow to cool. Peel the husks back from the corn and remove the silk. Slice off the corn kernels and set aside. Mince 2 cloves of garlic. Stir this in after the eggs have been added. The corn cheesecake is delicious garnished with the sliced red pepper!

Black Olive and Herb Cheesecake

This recipe is adapted from one by my friend Sharon Gutstadt. This is easy to make, and you can use any type of olive, sun-dried tomatoes, or artichokes in place of the black olives, as well as rosemary, parsley, or sage for the herbs. If you have a difficult time finding farmer cheese, you can just use all cottage cheese. This recipe can also be mixed by hand.

CRUST

1 tablespoon (14 g) butter, melted

½ cup (60 g) white sesame seeds

CHEESECAKE

1 cup (225 g) cottage cheese

1 cup (225 g) farmer cheese

3 tablespoons (24 g) all-purpose flour

3 large eggs

¾ cup (100 g) crumbled feta cheese

¾ cup (100 g) grated white cheddar cheese

½ cup (50 g) pitted finely chopped kalamata olives

½ teaspoon fresh thyme leaves

½ teaspoon kosher salt

Large pinch of ground black pepper

To make the crust: Pour the melted butter into the bottom of a 10-inch (25 cm) square baking pan. Using a pastry brush, brush butter all over the bottom and sides of the pan. Pour ⅓ cup (46 g) of the sesame seeds into the bottom of the pan and rotate the pan around so that the seeds cover the bottom and the sides completely; you will have a thin layer of seeds on the bottom. Set aside.

To make the cheesecake: Preheat the oven to 325ºF (170ºC, or gas mark 3).

In the bowl of an electric mixer, using the paddle attachment, mix the cottage cheese, farmer cheese, and flour on low speed until softened, scraping down the sides of the bowl, underneath the paddle, and the paddle frequently with a rubber spatula, about 1 minute. Add the eggs, one at a time, and mix just until combined, about 10 seconds after each egg. Add the feta, white cheddar, olives, thyme, salt, and pepper and mix on low just until combined.

Pour the batter over the crust and level with an offset spatula. Sprinkle the remaining sesame seeds on top of the batter. Place in the oven and bake for 30 to 40 minutes, until the cheesecake is firm in the center and lightly golden. Allow to cool for 1 hour before cutting.

To unmold, run a sharp knife or spatula around the edges of the pan. Using a small knife, cut the cheesecake into 2½-inch (6.4 cm) squares. Use a small offset spatula to lift the squares from the pan. Refrigerate until ready to serve.

Yield: One 10-inch (25 cm) square cheesecake

Variation: Mushroom Cheesecake

Use the same crust. Substitute diced mushrooms for the olives. Heat 1 tablespoon (14 g) butter in a large sauté pan until sizzling and hot. Add 1 cup (70 g) diced button mushrooms. Cook until the mushrooms are soft and golden brown, about 6 to 8 minutes. Remove from the heat and allow to cool completely before adding to the batter.

Minis, Pops, Bars, and Bites

Small and scrumptious, these are perfect for a party.
When entertaining, I like to make three or four
varieties so everyone can have a taste of each.
Of course, they are also perfect for everyday treats.

Salted Caramel Mini Cheesecakes

These adorable and delicious minis feature salt and caramel, one of my favorite flavor combinations. If your local grocery store doesn't carry *fleur de sel* (French for "flower of salt"), which is a specially harvested sea salt, a medium-grain sea salt can be substituted.

COOKIE CRUST

1 cup (50 g) finely ground cookies (about 16 vanilla wafers or gingersnaps)

3 tablespoons (42 g) unsalted butter, melted

CARAMEL SAUCE (makes 1¼ cups [300 ml])

1 cup (200 g) granulated sugar

¼ cup (60 ml) water

1 teaspoon lemon juice

4 tablespoons (55 g) unsalted butter

½ cup (120 ml) heavy cream

1 teaspoon *fleur de sel*

CHEESECAKE

8 ounces (225 g) mascarpone cheese

8 ounces (225 g) cream cheese

3 tablespoons (24 g) all-purpose flour

¼ cup (60 g) packed dark brown sugar

¼ cup (60 ml) caramel sauce, cooled

¼ cup (60 ml) heavy cream

2 large eggs

1 vanilla bean, split and scraped

GARNISH

1 cup (240 ml) caramel sauce

2 teaspoons (10 g) *fleur de sel*

To make the cookie crust: Preheat the oven to 350ºF (180ºC, or gas mark 4). Using the ingredients listed at left, follow the instructions on page 16 for making Simple Ground Crusts.

Line a 12-cup muffin pan with paper cupcake liners and place 1 heaping tablespoon (15 g) of the crust mixture in each one. Press the crumbs firmly into the bottom. Bake for about 10 minutes, or until solidified. Allow to cool completely, about 10 minutes.

To make the caramel sauce: In a medium 4-quart (4 L) saucepan (make sure you're using a saucepan with high sides, *not* a sauté pan or skillet), combine the granulated sugar, water, and lemon juice and cook over medium heat, stirring occasionally, until the sugar has dissolved. Using a pastry brush dipped in water, brush down any sugar crystals that are on the sides of the pan. Increase the heat to high and continue cooking, without stirring, brushing the sides of the pan with the wet pastry brush as needed. The caramel will begin to take on a light golden color. Gently swirl (but do *not* stir) the pan to evenly caramelize the sugar to a medium amber color. Remove from the heat and carefully add the butter, heavy cream, and *fleur de sel*. The mixture will begin to bubble and rise slightly in the pan. Whisk until smooth. Allow to cool completely, about 30 minutes.

To make the cheesecake: Lower the oven to 325ºF (170ºC, or gas mark 3).

In the bowl of an electric mixer, using the paddle attachment, mix the mascarpone, cream cheese, and flour on low speed until softened, scraping down the sides of the bowl, underneath the paddle, and the paddle frequently with a rubber spatula, about 2 minutes. Add the brown sugar and cooled caramel sauce and continue mixing on low while scraping down the sides, bottom, and paddle until there are no visible lumps. Pour in the heavy cream and mix just until combined. Add the eggs, one at a time, and mix just until combined, about 10 seconds for each egg. Stir in the vanilla bean seeds.

Pour ¼ cup (60 g) of the batter into each lined muffin cup. Place the filled pan on a baking tray. Put 2 cups (475 ml) hot water into a roasting pan. Place the muffin pan on the top rack and the roasting pan on the bottom rack. Bake for about 25 minutes, until the cheesecake is just firm. Turn the oven off, leaving the oven door ajar and the cheesecakes in the oven for 10 minutes. Remove from the oven and allow to cool at room temperature. Refrigerate for at least 4 hours to set completely.

To garnish: Gently lift each mini out of the pan with a small offset spatula. Discard the liners. Pour about 1 tablespoon (15 ml) of the caramel sauce on top of each cheesecake, and then sprinkle with a large pinch of *fleur de sel*. Refrigerate until ready to serve.

Yield: 12 mini cheesecakes

Cappuccino Nut Cheesecake Bars

In the early 1990s, when I worked in hotels, I made a cappuccino nut torte that everyone loved, and it sparked my desire to have a similar cheesecake. If you love coffee, then these delicate bars are for you. If you like a stronger coffee flavor, Kahlúa can be substituted for the Baileys or Frangelico in the recipe.

CRUST
Nut Crust made with almonds (page 17)

CHEESECAKE
2 tablespoons (16 g) instant espresso powder

2 tablespoons (30 ml) hot water

2 cups (480 g) sour cream

¾ cup (150 g) granulated sugar, divided

1½ pounds (680 g) cream cheese

8 ounces (225 g) mascarpone

½ cup (112 g) packed brown sugar

4 eggs

2 egg yolks

⅓ cup (80 ml) Bailey's Irish Cream

⅓ cup (80 ml) Frangelico

To make the crust: Preheat the oven to 350°F (180°C, or gas mark 4). Follow the instructions on page 17 for the Nut Crust, using almonds. Press into a 9 x 13-inch (23 x 33 cm) pan. Let cool completely before adding the cheesecake batter.

To make the cheesecake: Lower the oven to 325°F (170°C or gas mark 3).

In a small bowl, whisk together the instant espresso powder and hot water until completely dissolved; set aside.

In another small bowl, whisk together the sour cream and ½ cup (100 g) of the granulated sugar; set aside.

In the bowl of an electric mixer, using the paddle attachment, mix the cream cheese and mascarpone on low speed until softened, scraping down the sides of the bowl, underneath the paddle, and the paddle frequently with a rubber spatula, about 2 minutes. Add the remaining ¼ cup (50 g) granulated sugar and the brown sugar and continue mixing on low and scraping down the sides, bottom, and paddle until there are no visible lumps. Add the eggs, one at a time, and mix just until combined, about 10 seconds after each egg. Add in both yolks and stir just until combined, about 10 seconds. Stir in the Baileys, Frangelico, and instant espresso powder mixture.

Place the pan with the crust in a roasting pan (one that is around the same height or lower than your pan). Pour the batter over the almond crust and spread with a small offset spatula to level it. Place in the oven and pour almost boiling water into the roasting pan (it should come up halfway around the sides of the pan). Bake for about 50 minutes; remove from the oven and top with the sour cream mixture. Bake for another 10 minutes, until the cheesecake is firm around the edges, but still jiggly in the center (the jiggly part should be about the size of a quarter).

Remove from the oven and remove the cheesecake from the water bath. Gently run a small sharp knife or small spatula around the edges of the pan to loosen the cheesecake from the sides. Allow to cool at room temperature. Place in the refrigerator for at least 8 hours (this will help the cheesecake set completely). Remove from the refrigerator and slice into squares or rectangles to serve.

Yield: One 9 x 13-inch (23 x 33 cm) cheesecake

Variation: Espresso Brownie Cheesecake Bars

Omit the Baileys and Frangelico and substitute ⅓ cup (80 ml) strong brewed coffee and ⅓ cup (80 ml) Kahlúa. Use the Espresso Brownie Crust (page 20) instead of almond crust.

Cheesecake Pops

These are the ultimate in versatility; you can use any type of cheesecake with any type of cake to make very interesting combinations. Don't be afraid to experiment here—you cannot go wrong with these.

CHEESECAKE

4 cups (240 g) finely crumbled cake crumbs from Lemon or Red Velvet Cake (pages 18–19), divided

1½ cups (380 g) baked cheesecake

32 lollipop sticks (4- to 6-inch, or 10 to 15 cm)

OUTER COATING

1 pound (454 g) white, milk, or semisweet chocolate, finely chopped

2 tablespoon (30 ml) coconut oil or grapeseed oil

To the make the cheesecake: In a medium-size bowl, combine 3 cups (180 g) of the cake crumbs and the baked cheesecake and stir with a rubber spatula until completely combined. Using a small ice cream scoop, scoop 32 balls and use your palms to round into little balls. Place on a baking tray and place in the freezer until ready to use.

To make the outer coating: Place the chocolate and oil in a heatproof bowl. Set aside. Fill a medium-size saucepan with 1 inch (2.5 cm) of water and place over high heat to bring to a boil; turn the to low heat. Place the bowl of chocolate on top of the saucepan, stirring occasionally until melted. Remove from the heat and set aside.

To assemble, place the remaining 1 cup (60 g) cake crumbs on a plate; set aside. Remove the cake balls from the freezer.

Dip the end of the lollipop stick into the melted chocolate. Push the lollipop stick into the cake ball about halfway through. Place in the freezer or refrigerator to set the chocolate, about 2 minutes. Remove from the freezer and dip the cheesecake pops into the melted chocolate, shaking off the excess chocolate. Set these aside on a baking tray to harden. Once they are hard, dip the cheesecake pops in the melted chocolate again, shaking off the excess. Roll the cheesecake pops in the cake crumbs. Set aside to harden.

Yield: 32 pops

Crème Brûlée Cheesecakes

These are a play on cheesecakes. Part of the heavy cream in a traditional crème brûlée is substituted here with cream cheese, which provides a creamy smooth texture that I think is much better than the traditional version. To change the flavor, add up to 2 tablespoons (30 ml) of your favorite alcohol; rum, Grand Marnier, and framboise all work particularly well.

12 ounces (336 g) cream cheese

¼ cup plus 2 tablespoons (75 g) sugar, divided

1½ cups (355 ml) heavy cream

6 large egg yolks

2 teaspoons vanilla extract

Preheat the oven to 325ºF (170ºC or gas mark 3).

In the bowl of an electric mixer, using the paddle attachment, mix the cream cheese on low speed until softened, scraping down the sides of the bowl, underneath the paddle, and the paddle frequently with a rubber spatula, about 2 minutes.

Add ¼ cup (50 g) of the sugar and continue mixing on low and scraping down the sides, bottom, and paddle until there are no visible lumps. While the mixer is running on low, slowly pour in the heavy cream and mix just until combined. Add the egg yolks, one at a time, and mix just until combined, about 10 seconds after each egg. Stir in the vanilla.

Place 6 crème brûlée molds on a half sheet tray. Pour the mixture evenly among the molds. Place in the oven and pour almost boiling water onto the sheet tray (it should come up halfway around the sides of the molds). Bake for about 50 minutes, or until just set.

Remove from the oven and allow to cool to room temperature. Refrigerate for at least 2 hours.

When ready to serve, remove from the refrigerator and sprinkle each with 1 teaspoon of the remaining sugar. Using a butane torch, caramelize the sugar until golden brown. Alternatively, place the molds under a preheated broiler for 3 to 4 minutes.

Yield: 6 individual cheesecakes

Variation: Spiced Milk Chocolate Mini Cheesecakes

Place 4 ounces (112 g) milk chocolate in a heatproof bowl. Heat the heavy cream in a medium-size saucepan over high heat until just boiling; pour over the chocolate and whisk until smooth. Reduce the vanilla extract to 1 teaspoon, and add 1 teaspoon ground cinnamon and a pinch of cayenne.

Peanut Butter Chocolate Mini Cheesecakes

I love these little cheesecake cupcakes. I made them for a friend's son's birthday party instead of traditional cupcakes and they were a hit. Any nut butter or sunflower seed butter can be substituted for the peanut butter.

CRUST
Graham Cracker–Peanut Butter Crust (page 17)

CHEESECAKE
2 ounces (56 g) semisweet chocolate

2 tablespoons (30 ml) water

12 ounces (336 g) cream cheese

½ cup (100 g) sugar

½ cup (120 g) sour cream

2 large eggs

1 teaspoon vanilla extract

¼ cup (65 g) creamy unsalted peanut butter

GARNISH
¼ cup (35 g) coarsely chopped salted peanuts

To make the crust: Preheat the oven to 350ºF (180ºC, or gas mark 4). Follow the instructions on page 17 for the Graham Cracker–Peanut Butter Crust.

Line a 12-cup muffin pan with paper cupcake liners and place 1 heaping tablespoon (15 g) of the crust mixture in each one. Press the crumbs firmly into the bottom. Bake for about 10 minutes, or until solidified. Allow to cool completely, about 10 minutes.

To make the cheesecake: Lower the oven to 325ºF (170ºC, or gas mark 3).

In a small heatproof bowl, combine the chocolate and water and set aside. Fill a medium-size saucepan with 1 inch (2.5 cm) of water and place over high heat and bring to a boil. Reduce the heat to low. Place the bowl of chocolate on top of the saucepan, stirring occasionally until melted. Remove from the heat and allow to cool to room temperature.

Meanwhile, in the bowl of an electric mixer, using the paddle attachment, mix the cream cheese on low speed until softened, scraping down the sides of the bowl, underneath the paddle, and the paddle frequently with a rubber spatula, about 2 minutes. Add the sugar and continue mixing on low and scraping down the sides, bottom, and paddle until there are no visible lumps. Add the sour cream and mix for 1 minute. Add the eggs, one at a time, and mix just until combined, about 10 seconds after each egg. Stir in the vanilla.

Divide the batter evenly between two bowls. Into one bowl, whisk in the cooled melted chocolate until smooth and completely combined. Into the other bowl, whisk in the peanut butter until smooth and completely combined.

Divide the peanut butter batter evenly among the lined muffin cups. Divide the chocolate batter evenly over the peanut butter batter. Place the filled pan on a baking tray. Put 2 cups (475 ml) hot water into a roasting pan. Place the muffin pan on the top rack and the roasting pan on the bottom rack. Bake for about 50 minutes, until the cheesecake is firm around the edges, but but is still jiggly in the center (the jiggly part should be about the size of a quarter).

Remove from the oven and allow to cool at room temperature. Refrigerate for at least 4 hours (this will help the cheesecake set completely).

To garnish: Gently lift each mini out of the pan with a small, offset spatula and garnish with the chopped peanuts.

Yield: 12 mini cheesecakes

Variation:
Almond Butter and White Chocolate Mini Cheesecakes

Substitute white chocolate for the semisweet chocolate and almond butter for the peanut butter. Substitute toasted chopped almonds for the peanuts.

Matcha Cheesecake Bars with Black Sesame Crust

This is a perfect afternoon snack. The subtle flavor of green tea is a wonderful match with the Black Sesame Seed Crust. Other tea powders can be used instead of green tea.

CRUST

Sesame Seed Sweet Dough Crust variation
  (page 22)

CHEESECAKE

2 pounds (908 g) cream cheese

1 cup (200 g) sugar

2 tablespoons (16 g) cornstarch

1 tablespoon (8 g) matcha green tea powder

¼ cup (80 g) honey

1 cup (240 g) whole milk plain yogurt

1 cup (240 ml) heavy cream

4 large eggs

To make the crust: Preheat the oven to 350ºF (180ºC, or gas mark 4). Follow the instructions on page 22 for the Sesame Seed Sweet Dough Crust variation. Place in a 9 x 13-inch (23 x 33 cm) pan. Let cool completely before adding the cheesecake batter.

To make the cheesecake: Lower the oven to 325ºF (170ºC, or gas mark 3).

In the bowl of an electric mixer, using the paddle attachment, mix the cream cheese on low speed until softened, scraping down the sides of the bowl, underneath the paddle, and the paddle frequently with a rubber spatula, about 2 minutes. Add the sugar, cornstarch, and matcha green tea powder; continue mixing on low and scraping down the sides, bottom, and paddle until there are no visible lumps. Add the honey and mix just until combined, about 1 minute. While the mixer is running, add the yogurt and heavy cream, and mix for 1 minute. Scrape down the sides of the bowl. Add the eggs, one at a time, and mix just until combined, about 10 seconds after each egg.

Place the pan with the crust in a roasting pan (one that is around the same height or lower than your pan). Pour the batter over the crust and level it with a small offset spatula. Place in the oven and pour almost boiling water into the roasting pan (it should come up halfway around the sides of the pan). Bake for about 1 hour 10 minutes, or until the cheesecake is firm around the edges, but still jiggly in the center (the jiggly part should be about the size of a quarter).

Remove from the oven and remove the cheesecake from the water bath. Gently run a small sharp knife or small spatula around the edges of the pan to loosen the cheesecake from the sides. Allow to cool at room temperature. Place in the refrigerator for at least 8 hours (this will help the cheesecake set completely). Remove from the refrigerator and slice into squares to serve.

Yield: One 9 x 13 inch (23 x 33 cm) cheesecake

Variation: Acai Cheesecake Bars

Substitute 1 tablespoon (8 g) acai powder for the green tea powder.

Cheesecake Truffles

These are great to make if you have any leftover cheesecake, but that's not likely. You can use any baked cheesecake recipe in this book to make these, and they are a wonderful gift!

TRUFFLES

3 cups (720 g) baked cheesecake, chilled

OUTER COATING

1 pound (454 g) white, milk, or semisweet chocolate, finely chopped

2 tablespoons (30 ml) coconut oil or grapeseed oil

2 cups (240 g) graham cracker crumbs, cookie crumbs, cocoa powder, flaked coconut, or chopped toasted nuts

To the make the truffles: Using a small ice cream scoop, scoop about 1- to 1½-tablespoon (15 to 23 g) balls and use your palms to round into little balls. Place on a baking tray and place in the freezer until ready to use.

To make the outer coating: Place the chocolate and oil in a heatproof bowl. Set aside. Fill a medium-size saucepan with 1 inch (2.5 cm) of water and place over high heat to bring to a boil; turn the heat to low. Place the bowl of chocolate on top of the saucepan, stirring occasionally until melted. Remove from the heat and set aside.

Spread the graham cracker crumbs or other coatings in a baking pan. Using a fork, dip the truffles in the melted chocolate, making sure all sides are coated and shaking off the excess chocolate. Place the truffle in the pan and roll to coat. Remove from the crumbs and chill until ready to serve.

Variation: Chocolate-Covered Cheesecake Squares

Bake any cheesecake, without a crust, in a 9- or 10-inch (23 or 25 cm) square springform pan as directed. Once the cheesecake has been refrigerated for at least 8 hours, unmold from the pan and place in the freezer for about 2 hours. Remove from the freezer and cut the cheesecake into 1-inch (2.5 cm) squares. Dip in chocolate as directed above.

Lemon Cheesecake Bars

This recipe is based on my friend and cookbook author Cara Tannenbaum's delicious lemon bar recipe. You can always substitute any other citrus in place of the lemon.

CRUST
Sweet Dough Crust (page 22)

CHEESECAKE
3 large lemons

5 eggs

2 cups (400 g) sugar

4 ounces (112 g) cream cheese

½ cup (120 g) sour cream

To make the crust: Preheat the oven to 350ºF (180ºC, or gas mark 4). Follow the instructions on page 22 for the Sweet Dough Crust. Place in a 9 x 13-inch (23 x 33 cm) pan. Let cool completely before adding the cheesecake batter.

To make the cheesecake: Lower the oven to 325ºF (170ºC, or gas mark 3). Finely grate the zest from the lemons, taking care not to include any of the white pith. Set aside. Squeeze the lemons to make 3 ounces (90 ml) of fresh juice, straining out the seeds. In a mixing bowl, beat the eggs well. Add the sugar, lemon juice, and the zest. Beat just until combined. Set aside.

In the bowl of an electric mixer, using the paddle attachment, mix the cream cheese on low speed until softened, scraping down the sides of the bowl, underneath the paddle, and the paddle frequently with a rubber spatula, about 2 minutes. Add the sour cream and mix for another 30 seconds, or until just combined. Add the lemon/egg mixture and mix for 1 minute or until just combined.

Place the pan with the crust in a roasting pan (one that is around the same height or lower than your pan). Pour the batter over crust and level it with a small offset spatula. Place in the oven and pour almost boiling water into the roasting pan (it should come up halfway around the sides of the pan). Bake for about 1 hour 10 minutes, until the cheesecake is firm around the edges, but still jiggly in the center (the jiggly part should be about the size of a quarter).

Remove from the oven and remove cheesecake from the water bath. Gently run a small sharp knife or small spatula around the edges of the pan to loosen the cheesecake from the sides. Allow to cool at room temperature. Place in the refrigerator for at least 8 hours (this will help the cheesecake set completely). Remove from the refrigerator and slice into squares to serve.

Yield: One 9 x 13 inch (23 x 33 cm) cheesecake

No-Bake Cheesecakes

No-bake cheesecakes are perfect if you don't have time to wait for them to set up. Some no-bakes are ready immediately; others, which have gelatin, require just a few hours to set up. Another plus is they don't require an oven, so they are the perfect summertime dessert.

Black-Bottom Cheesecake Bars

This recipe is based on black bottom pie, which is a chocolate crust, layers of chocolate and vanilla puddings, and whipped cream. Here, I use cream cheese as well as milk for the custard. The crust needs to be doubled here so it is thick enough to support the custard. Although these take a little more time to make, they are well worth it!

CRUST

2 batches Cookie Crust made with chocolate sandwich cookies (page 17)

CHEESECAKE CUSTARD

3 cups (705 ml) milk, divided

1 tablespoon (8 g) granulated gelatin

¾ cup plus 2 tablespoons (175 g) sugar, divided

3 large eggs

3 tablespoons (24 g) cornstarch

6 ounces (170 g) cream cheese

1 tablespoon (15 ml) vanilla extract

6 ounces (170 g) semisweet chocolate, finely chopped

2 cups (470 ml) heavy cream, cold

GARNISH

1 cup (100 g) chocolate shavings (page 150)

To make the crust: Preheat the oven to 350ºF (180ºC, or gas mark 4). Follow the instructions on page 17 for the Cookie Crust, using chocolate sandwich cookies. Place in a 9 x 13-inch (23 x 33 cm) pan. Let cool completely before adding the cheesecake custard.

To make the cheesecake custard: In a small bowl, combine ¼ cup (60 ml) of the milk and the gelatin; set aside.

In a medium-size saucepan, whisk together the remaining 2¾ cups (645 ml) milk and ½ cup (100 g) of the sugar. Place over medium-high heat and cook, stirring occasionally, until the sugar dissolves, 2 to 3 minutes. Remove from the heat.

Meanwhile, in a medium-size heatproof bowl, whisk together ¼ cup (50 g) sugar, the eggs, and the cornstarch until completely combined. Slowly whisk half of the milk mixture into the eggs. Place the egg mixture back in the saucepan with the milk. Place over medium heat and cook, whisking constantly, until the mixture comes to a boil and thickens slightly, 4 to 5 minutes. Remove the mixture from the heat and whisk in the cream cheese and vanilla until completely combined.

Remove 1 cup (240 g) of the mixture and place in a small heatproof bowl; immediately add the chocolate and whisk until completely combined and the chocolate is melted; set aside.

Add the milk and gelatin mixture to the bowl of vanilla batter and whisk until combined; set aside to cool.

Meanwhile, in the bowl of an electric mixer, with the whip attachment, combine the heavy cream and remaining 2 tablespoons (25 g) sugar and beat on medium-high speed, 4 to 6 minutes, until stiff peaks form. Divide the whipped cream in half and add half to the cooled vanilla mixture. Using a rubber spatula, gently fold in the whipped cream by cutting down the center of the mixture with the wide side of the spatula, lifting the mixture up, and turning over. Rotate the bowl 90 degrees and continue folding until the whipped cream is (just) fully incorporated.

Pour the chocolate mixture on top of the crust and use a small offset spatula to spread so that the mixture reaches the edges of the pan and is smooth and level on top. Pour on the vanilla mixture, and again spread it to the edges and until smooth and level. Top with the remaining whipped cream and chocolate shavings. Allow to cool at room temperature. Place in the refrigerator for at least 4 hours (this will help the cheesecake set completely). Remove from the refrigerator and slice into squares to serve.

Yield: One 9 x 13 inch (23 x 33 cm) cheesecake

Variation: Black Bottom Mint Cheesecake Bars

Substitute mint extract for the vanilla.

Blueberry Cheesecake Trifle

I use a trifle bowl to assemble this, but individual glasses can be used as well. You will have one leftover cake layer from the recipe. It can be frozen for later use.

CRUST
Double the Lemon Cake Crust recipe (page 18)

CHEESECAKE FILLING
1 pound (454 g) cream cheese

½ cup (100 g) sugar

½ cup (120 g) sour cream

½ cup (120 g) crème fraîche

1 vanilla bean, split and scraped, or
  2 teaspoons vanilla extract

1 tablespoon (6 g) lemon zest

3 tablespoons (45 ml) cold water, divided

1½ teaspoons granulated gelatin

LAYERS
¾ cup (180 g) blueberry jam

2 pints (580 g) fresh blueberries, picked over
  and cleaned

1 cup (240 ml) heavy cream, whipped (page 150)

To make cheesecake filling: In the bowl of an electric mixer, using the paddle attachment, mix the cream cheese on medium speed until softened, scraping down the sides of the bowl, underneath the paddle, and the paddle frequently with a rubber spatula, about 2 minutes. Add the sugar and continue mixing on medium and scraping down the sides, bottom, and paddle until there are no visible lumps. Add the sour cream and crème fraîche and mix for 1 minute. Add the vanilla and lemon zest and stir to combine. Set aside.

Put 1 tablespoon (15 ml) of the cold water in a small bowl. Evenly sprinkle the gelatin on top (make sure the gelatin does not clump) and set aside for about 5 minutes. Meanwhile, place the remaining 2 tablespoons (30 ml) water in a small saucepan and heat over medium-high heat until simmering (alternatively, heat in the microwave) and then pour over the gelatin. Stir or whisk until the gelatin is dissolved. Immediately pour this mixture into the cream cheese mixture and whisk until combined.

To make the layers: Using a serrated knife, slice each layer in half horizontally. Set aside. Place a layer of the cake inside the trifle bowl. If you have a smaller bowl, trim the cake to fit. Pour ¼ cup (60 g) of the blueberry jam on the top of the cake and use an offset spatula to spread it to the edge of the trifle bowl. Place 1 cup (145 g) of the blueberries in a single layer on top of the jam. Add approximately half of the cheesecake filling (about 2 cups, or 480 g). Repeat the layering one more time. Repeat layering with the cake, jam, and blueberries, and then top with the whipped cream. This can be served immediately or refrigerated for up to 3 days.

Yield: One 9-inch (23 cm) trifle

Variation: Three-Berry Cheesecake Trifle

Use raspberry jam instead of blueberry jam. Use 1 pint (340 g) quartered strawberries and 1 pint (290 g) blackberries instead of blueberries.

Buttermilk Chocolate Almond Chia Cheesecake

This recipe is tangy with the buttermilk. If you prefer, you can substitute whole milk. If you like it even sweeter, you can also add up to ⅓ cup (40 g) confectioners' sugar when mixing the cream cheese.

CHEESECAKE

2 cups (470 ml) buttermilk, divided

4 ounces (112 g) semisweet chocolate, finely chopped

1 pound (454 g) cream cheese

¼ cup (42 g) chia seeds

1 tablespoon (15 ml) almond extract

GARNISH

Whipped cream or Whipped Coconut Cream (page 150 or 151)

2 tablespoons (16 g) cocoa nibs (optional)

In a medium-size heatproof bowl, combine ½ cup (120 ml) of the buttermilk and the semisweet chocolate. Set aside. Fill a medium-size saucepan with 1 inch (2.5 cm) of water and place over high heat and bring to a boil. Reduce the heat to low. Place the bowl of chocolate on top of the saucepan, stirring occasionally until melted. Remove from the heat and allow to cool, stirring occasionally, until no longer warm to the touch.

Meanwhile, place the cream cheese in the bowl of a food processor and process for 1 minute on high speed. Stop the food processor and scrape down the sides of the bowl. Process for another minute. Add the remaining 1½ cups (350 ml) buttermilk, melted chocolate mixture, chia seeds, and almond extract and process on high until completely combined and smooth, about 2 minutes.

Remove from the food processor and divide evenly among 6 serving cups. Refrigerate for at least 4 hours.

To garnish: Serve with a dollop of whipped cream or Whipped Coconut Cream and sprinkle with cocoa nibs, if desired.

Yield: 6 individual servings

Cannoli Cheesecake

My favorite part of the cannoli is the filling, so this is just perfect—a little crust, but mostly filling. I like mini chocolate chips in my filling, but you can substitute candied fruit.

CRUST

Cookie Crust Citrus variation made with graham crackers or Chocolate Sweet Dough Crust variation (page 16 or 22)

CHEESECAKE

¼ cup (60 ml) water

1 tablespoon (8 g) granulated gelatin

¼ cup (60 ml) milk

1½ pounds (680 g) ricotta

8 ounces (225 g) cream cheese

2 cups (240 g) confectioners' sugar

1 tablespoon (15 ml) vanilla extract

1 teaspoon ground cinnamon

1 teaspoon orange zest

¾ cup (130 g) mini chocolate chips, divided

GARNISH

Candied Orange Peel (page 149, optional)

To make the crust: Preheat the oven to 350ºF (180ºC, or gas mark 4). Follow the instructions on page 16 or 22 for the Cookie Crust Citrus Variation made with graham crackers or Chocolate Sweet Dough Crust variation. Let cool completely before adding the cheesecake.

To make the cheesecake: In a medium-size bowl, combine the water and granulated gelatin; set aside for 2 to 3 minutes.

In a small saucepan, heat the milk over medium heat until hot, but not boiling (steam should be coming off the milk), pour over the gelatin, and whisk until smooth. Cool until just barely warm to the touch. Set aside.

Meanwhile, in a food processor, combine the ricotta and cream cheese and process until smooth and creamy, about 2 minutes. Add the confectioners' sugar and process until completely combined, about 1 minute. Scrape down the sides of the bowl. Add the vanilla, cinnamon, and orange zest and process for 30 seconds until combined. Remove from the food processor and place in a medium-size bowl. Whisk in the gelatin mixture until completely combined.

Sprinkle ½ cup (85 g) of the chocolate chips on top of the crust. Top with the cheesecake mixture and spread with an offset spatula to smooth and level it. Place in the refrigerator and chill for at least 4 hours, until the cheesecake is firm.

To garnish: Garnish with the remaining ¼ cup (45 g) mini chocolate chips and candied orange peel.

Yield: One 10-inch (25 cm) cheesecake

Variation: Cherry Blossom Cheesecake

Omit the vanilla, cinnamon, and orange zest and add 1½ teaspoons cherry blossom flavor.

Coffee-Toffee Cheesecake Parfaits

My dad, Charles, loves toffee, coffee, and cheesecake, and this is for him. I like to make my own toffee, but you can also use store-bought and grind it in a food processor. Another great substitute for toffee is nut brittle (page 152).

TOFFEE

1 cup (225 g) butter

¾ cup (150 g) sugar

¼ cup (60 ml) maple syrup

2 tablespoons (40 g) molasses

1 cup (175 g) chocolate chips

4 ounces (112 g) sliced toasted almonds

CHEESECAKE

12 ounces (336 g) cream cheese

12 ounces (336 g) mascarpone

¼ cup (55 g) light brown sugar

1 cup (240 ml) sweetened condensed milk

1 tablespoon (15 ml) Kahlúa

1 tablespoon (8 g) instant espresso powder

⅛ teaspoon ground cinnamon

To make the toffee: Line a cookie tray with foil and set aside.

In a medium-size saucepan, combine the butter, sugar, maple syrup, and molasses. Stirring constantly, cook to 300ºF (150ºC), the hard crack stage, on a candy thermometer. Pour onto the foil and set aside to cool to lukewarm.

Scatter the chocolate chips on the toffee and spread with an offset spatula. The chips should melt and spread easily. Sprinkle with the toasted almonds and allow to cool completely.

Once cooled completely, place in a food processor and pulse the mixture until coarsely ground. Remove from the food processor and set aside.

To make the cheesecake: In a food processor, combine the cream cheese and mascarpone until smooth and creamy, about 2 minutes. Add the brown sugar and process until completely combined, about 1 minute. Scrape down the sides of the bowl. Add the condensed milk, Kahlúa, espresso powder, and cinnamon and process for about 1 minute, until combined.

To assemble, in each of 6 parfait glasses, put 2 tablespoons (16 g) of ground toffee in each glass. Pour in about ⅓ cup (80 g) of the cheesecake mixture; layer 2 tablespoons (16 g) ground toffee, then pour in another ⅓ cup (80 g) cheesecake mixture; top with some ground toffee. Refrigerate for at least 2 hours before serving.

Yield: 6 individual servings

Variation: Rocky Road Cheesecake Parfaits

In the toffee, omit the almonds and substitute walnuts. In the cheesecake mixture, omit the Kahlúa and instant espresso powder and add 2 tablespoons (16 g) cocoa powder. When assembling, garnish with mini marshmallows.

Silken Tofu Cheesecake

This recipe is from my friend, Japanese cookbook author Aiko Tanaka. The texture of this cheesecake is similar to panna cotta, and using the yogurt and tofu with the cream cheese provides a delicate flavor. It's easy to change the flavor of this by using your favorite fruit juice in place of the orange juice.

CRUST
Any variation of a chocolate crust
    (pages 17 to 22)

CHEESECAKE
2 tablespoons (30 ml) water

1 tablespoon (10 g) granulated gelatin

½ cup (120 ml) orange juice

6 tablespoons (90 ml) white wine

1 cup (200 g) sugar

7 ounces (200 g) silken tofu

7 ounces (200 g) cream cheese

7 ounces (200 g) whole milk plain yogurt

7 ounces (200 g) heavy cream, whipped

GARNISH
Winter Version Compote (page 146)

To make the crust: Preheat the oven to 350°F (180°C, or gas mark 4). Follow the instructions (pages 17 to 22) for any chocolate crust variation. Press into a 9 x 13-inch (23 x 33 cm) pan. Let cool completely before adding the cheesecake batter.

To make the cheesecake: In a medium-size bowl, combine the water and granulated gelatin and set aside for 2 to 3 minutes.

In a medium-size saucepan, combine the orange juice, white wine, and sugar and cook over medium heat, stirring occasionally, until the sugar is dissolved, about 5 minutes. Remove from the heat and pour over the gelatin. Whisk until smooth. Allow to cool completely.

Combine the tofu, cream cheese, and yogurt in the bowl of a food processer. Process until smooth, about 2 minutes.

Whisk together the tofu and orange juice mixtures. Place the heavy cream in the bowl of an electric mixer. Using the whip attachment beat on medium speed until stiff peaks begin to form. Using a rubber spatula, add all of the whipped cream to the tofu mixture and begin to fold in by cutting down the center of the mixture with the spatula, lifting the mixture up, and turning over. Rotate the bowl 90 degrees and repeat until the whipped cream is fully incorporated. Fold in the whipped cream. Pour over the crust and chill for at least 1 hour.

To garnish: Slice into squares and garnish with the compote.

Yield: One 9 x 13 inch (23 x 33 cm) cheesecake

Frozen Banana Split Cheesecake Parfaits

Although I love these frozen—and they taste just like layers of chocolate, vanilla, and strawberry ice cream when they are—if you don't have room in your freezer or just don't want to freeze them, you can refrigerate them for a softer texture.

CHEESECAKE

1½ pounds (680 g) cream cheese

¾ cup (180 ml) sweetened condensed milk

1 teaspoon vanilla extract

1 ½ tablespoons (12 g) cocoa powder, sifted

3 tablespoons (45 g) strawberry jam

3 bananas, peeled and sliced into ¼-inch (6 mm) pieces

GARNISH

¼ cup (60 ml) Whipped Cream (page 150)

6 tablespoons (54 g) chopped, toasted walnuts

To make the cheesecake: In a food processor, add the cream cheese and condensed milk; process until smooth and creamy, about 2 minutes. Scrape down the sides of the bowl. Remove the mixture from the food processor and divide evenly (about 1¼ cups [300 g], each) among 3 separate bowls. In one bowl stir in the vanilla extract. In the second bowl, stir in the cocoa powder, and in the third bowl stir in the strawberry jam, mixing each until completely combined.

To assemble, in each of 6 parfait glasses, pour about ¼ cup (60 g) of the vanilla layer. Place 4 or 5 slices of banana on top. Pour in about ¼ cup (60 g) of the chocolate and layer with 4 or 5 slices of banana. Pour in about ¼ cup (60 g) of the strawberry. Freeze until ready to serve, or refrigerate for at least 2 hours before serving.

To make the garnish: Just before serving, top with a dollop of whipped cream and sprinkle each with 1 tablespoon (9 g) of the walnuts.

Yield: 6 individual servings

Pistachio Cheesecake

This has a gorgeous color from the pistachios, but you can substitute different nuts, such as pecans, hazelnuts, or macadamia nuts, to change the flavor of this cheesecake.

CRUST

Cookie Crust made with graham crackers (page 17)

PISTACHIO PASTE

1 cup (145 g) unsalted shelled pistachios

¼ cup (50 g) sugar

CHEESECAKE

1½ cups (355 ml) heavy cream

1 pound (454 g) cream cheese

8 ounces (225 g) fromage blanc

½ cup (100 g) sugar

1 tablespoon (15 ml) lemon juice

1 teaspoon lemon zest

1½ tablespoons (12 g) gelatin

¼ cup (60 ml) water

GARNISH

½ cup (75 g) chopped pistachios

To make the crust: Preheat the oven to 350ºF (180ºC, or gas mark 4). Follow the instructions on page 17 for the Cookie Crust, using graham crackers. Let cool completely before adding the cheesecake batter.

To make the pistachio paste: Place the pistachios and sugar in the bowl of a food processor. Grind together, scraping down the sides of the bowl occasionally, until the pistachios are a paste, 4 to 5 minutes. Set aside.

To make the cheesecake: Place the heavy cream in the bowl of an electric mixer with the whip attachment and beat on medium-high speed until the cream begins to thicken and hold its shape. Reduce the speed to medium and continue to beat until the cream has a stiff peak, being careful not to over whip. Set aside.

In the bowl of an electric mixer, using the paddle attachment, mix the cream cheese, fromage blanc, and sugar on medium speed until softened, scraping down the sides of the bowl, underneath the paddle, and the paddle occasionally with a rubber spatula, about 2 minutes. Add the pistachio paste and mix for about 1 minute until combined. Add the lemon juice and zest and mix until just combined, about 30 seconds. Set aside.

In a small heatproof bowl, combine the gelatin and water and allow to sit for 3 minutes. Fill a medium-size saucepan with 1 inch (2.5 cm) of water and place over high heat and bring to a boil. Reduce the heat to low. Place the bowl of gelatin on top of the saucepan, stirring occasionally until the gelatin has dissolved. Remove from the heat and beat the gelatin into the pistachio mixture.

Using a large rubber spatula, add half of the whipped cream and begin to fold in by cutting down the center of the mixture with the wide side of the spatula, lifting the mixture up, and turning over. Rotate the bowl 90 degrees and repeat one more time. Add the remaining whipped cream and continue folding until the cream is just fully incorporated. Pour the batter over the crust and spread with a small offset spatula to level it. Refrigerate for at least 4 hours before serving.

To garnish: Sprinkle the chopped pistachios over the top just before serving.

Yield: One 10-inch (25 cm) cheesecake

Variation: Pine Nut Cheesecake

Use the Chocolate Sweet Dough Crust (page 22). Substitute pine nuts for the pistachios in the paste and garnish. Place the pine nuts on a cookie sheet and toast in a preheated 325ºF (170ºC, or gas mark 3) oven for about 20 minutes, or until golden brown, stirring occasionally. Remove from the oven and allow to cool slightly. Proceed as directed above.

Coconut Cream Cheesecake Parfaits

If your favorite candy bar, like mine, involves chocolate, almonds, and coconut, then you will love this sublime, layered cheesecake. For a variation, try using white chocolate instead of semisweet.

CHEESECAKE

¼ cup (60 ml) water, divided

2 ¼ teaspoons granulated gelatin

2 pounds (908 g) cream cheese

½ cup (100 g) sugar

1 can (15 ounces, or 420 g) cream of coconut

¼ cup (60 ml) coconut milk

2 teaspoons coconut extract

1 tablespoon (15 ml) spiced or gold rum

¾ cup (64 g) toasted coconut, plus extra for garnish

¾ cup (110 g) chopped toasted almonds

COCONUT CHOCOLATE SAUCE

3 ounces (84 g) semisweet chocolate

6 tablespoons (90 ml) coconut milk

1 teaspoon coconut extract

To make the cheesecake: In a medium-size bowl, combine 2 tablespoons (30 ml) of the water and the granulated gelatin; set aside for 2 to 3 minutes.

In a small saucepan, heat the remaining 2 tablespoons (30 ml) water over high heat until just boiling, pour over the gelatin, and whisk until smooth. Set aside.

In a food processor, combine the cream cheese and sugar and process until smooth and creamy, about 2 minutes. Add the cream of coconut, coconut milk, coconut extract, and rum, and process until completely combined, about 1 minute. Scrape down the sides of the bowl. Remove from the food processor and place in a medium-size bowl. Whisk in the gelatin mixture until completely combined.

To make the coconut chocolate sauce: In a medium-size heatproof bowl, combine the chocolate and coconut milk. Set aside. Fill a medium-size saucepan with 1 inch (2.5 cm) of water and place over high heat and bring to a boil. Reduce the heat to low. Place the bowl of chocolate on top of the saucepan, stirring occasionally until melted. Remove from the heat, stir in the coconut extract, and allow to cool. Keep this at room temperature and assemble immediately, or the chocolate will become too firm.

To assemble, in each of 6 parfait glasses, layer 1 tablespoon (15 ml) of the coconut chocolate sauce, about ⅓ cup (80 g) of the cheesecake mixture, 2 tablespoons (10 g) of the toasted coconut, another ⅓ cup (80 g) of the cheesecake mixture, 2 tablespoons (10 g) of the toasted almonds, another ⅓ cup (80 g) of the cheesecake mixture, and 1 tablespoon (15 ml) of the chocolate sauce. Refrigerate for at least 2 hours before serving.

To garnish: Lightly garnish with toasted coconut and serve.

Yield: 6 individual servings

Tiramisu Cheesecake

This is a close cousin to tiramisu, but better. This recipe uses half cream cheese and half mascarpone and the best part is that it has no eggs! If you aren't a coffee fan, or just want to change the flavor, omit the coffee and substitute orange juice and omit the Kahlúa and substitute Grand Marnier.

1 pound (454 g) cream cheese

1 pound (454 g) mascarpone

1½ cups (300 g) sugar

2 teaspoons vanilla extract

1 cup (235 ml) brewed coffee

¼ cup (60 ml) Kahlúa

1 teaspoon instant espresso powder

¼ cup (60 ml) heavy cream

13 ladyfingers

1 cup (130 g) grated chocolate (page 150), divided

GARNISH
2 tablespoons (16 g) cocoa powder

In a food processor, combine the cream cheese and mascarpone and process until smooth and creamy, about 1 minute. Add the sugar and vanilla and process until completely combined, about 1 minute. Scrape down the sides of the bowl and process for another 30 seconds. Remove from the food processor and divide the mixture evenly between 2 bowls.

In a small bowl, combine the coffee, Kahlúa, and instant espresso powder. Add ¼ cup (60 ml) of the mixture to one bowl of cream cheese and mix until completely combined; set aside. Add the heavy cream to the other bowl of cream cheese and mix until completely combined; set aside.

Spread the cream cheese/Kahlúa mixture on the bottom of a 9-inch (23 cm) square baking dish. Dip both sides of the ladyfingers into the remaining 1 cup (235 ml) coffee/Kahlúa mixture and place on top. Sprinkle with ½ cup (65 g) of the grated chocolate. Spread the cream cheese/heavy cream mixture on top. Sprinkle with the remaining ½ cup (65 g) grated chocolate. Chill until ready to serve.

To garnish: Dust lightly with cocoa powder before serving.

Variation: Irish Cream Cheesecake

Substitute Bailey's Irish Cream for the Kahlúa.

Presentations and Garnishes

The final finishes that will make all of your cheesecakes look as tempting as they will taste.

Fruit Sauces and Sides

Fruit Sauce

For these sauces, you can use any type of berry. If you use raspberries, use a fine strainer to remove the seeds. The amount of sugar should be adjusted depending on your personal taste and the sweetness of the fruit.

1 pound (454 g) fresh or frozen berries, quartered

¼ to ⅓ cup (50 to 70 g) sugar

1 tablespoon (15 ml) lemon juice (optional)

In a medium-size saucepan, combine the berries, ¼ cup (50 g) of the sugar, and the lemon juice, if using; cook over medium heat until the berries are softened, about 5 minutes. Taste the sauce and adjust the sugar if necessary. If you need to add more sugar, reheat the sauce until the sugar is completely dissolved. Remove from the heat and allow to cool completely. Place in a blender or food processor and process until completely smooth. Strain to remove any seeds. Refrigerate for up to 2 weeks.

Yield: 1½ cups (360 g)

Fresh Fruit Compote

This versatile compote can be made with almost any fresh fruit. I like to choose what is in season; in the winter, I use all citrus. In the summer, I use berries, peaches, plums, and nectarines, but the possibilities are endless. I also like to leave the skin on fruits, but they can be peeled, if desired. It is used in the Silken Tofu Cheesecake (page 135), but can really be served with almost any cheesecake.

WINTER VERSION

4 blood oranges or 2 pink grapefruit, peeled and sliced into segments

4 kiwi, peeled and sliced into eighths

2 oranges, peeled and sliced into segments

2 to 4 tablespoons (25 to 50 g) sugar

SUMMER VERSION

2 peaches, pitted and diced

2 plums, pitted and diced

1 cup (125 g) raspberries

2 to 4 tablespoons (25 to 50 g) sugar

2 to 4 tablespoons (30 to 60 ml) orange liqueur or orange juice

In a medium-size bowl, mix all the ingredients and refrigerate for at least 1 hour before serving.

Yield: 2 cups (500 g)

Dried Fruit Compote

This is a great alternative to fresh fruits and pairs beautifully with the Vegan Cashew Vanilla Bean Cheesecake (page 57).

2 cups (470 ml) apple cider or cranberry juice

1 cup (145 g) dried cherries

8 dried apricots, diced

8 pitted prunes, diced

2 tablespoons (30 ml) lemon juice

1 cinnamon stick

In a medium-size saucepan, combine all of the ingredients and cook over medium heat until the mixture is syrupy and the fruit is soft, 15 to 17 minutes. Remove from the heat; allow to cool slightly, then remove the cinnamon stick.

Yield: 2 cups (500 g)

Fruit Purées

These purées are used in the Brown Sugar Peach Cheesecake (page 78), Blackberry Cheesecake variation (page 79), and the Mascarpone and Raspberry Cheesecake (page 82)

BERRY PURÉE

1½ cups (235 g) raspberries, blackberries, or quartered strawberries, fresh or frozen (defrost if using frozen)

2 tablespoons (24 g) sugar

In a medium-size saucepan, combine the berries and sugar over medium-high heat. Cook, stirring occasionally, until the berries are softened, about 5 to 7 minutes. Remove from the heat and allow to cool slightly, about 5 minutes. Place in a food processor and purée until smooth. Remove from the processor and pour into a fine strainer set over a bowl. Use a ladle to push the purée through the strainer, discarding the seeds. Refrigerate the purée for up to 5 days or freeze for up to 2 months.

Yield: About 1 cup (250 g)

STONE FRUIT PURÉE

1 pound (640 g) peeled, pitted, and chopped stone fruit, fresh or frozen (defrosted)

2 tablespoons (24 g) sugar

2 tablespoons (30 ml) water

In a medium-size saucepan, combine the fruit, sugar, and water over medium-high heat. Cook, stirring occasionally, until the fruit is softened and beginning to break down, about 8 to 10 minutes. Remove from the heat and allow to cool slightly. Place in a food processor and purée until smooth. Remove from the processor and pour into a strainer set over a bowl. Use a ladle to push the purée through the strainer. Refrigerate for up to 5 days or freeze for up to 2 months.

Yield: About 1 cup (250 g)

Sautéed Pineapple

I love to serve this warm fruit with the Saffron Cheesecake (page 58). The contrast in the temperatures is quite pleasing. Any type of fruit can be substitute for the pineapple.

2 tablespoons (28 g) unsalted butter

½ large pineapple, peeled, cored, and diced

1 vanilla bean, split and scraped

Pinch of good-quality saffron

1 tablespoon (15 g) light brown sugar

⅛ teaspoon coarse sea salt

Pinch of ground black pepper

Melt the butter in a large sauté pan over high heat. Add the pineapple, vanilla bean, and saffron. Cook until the pineapple is slightly softened, about 5 minutes. Add the brown sugar, salt, and pepper. Cook for about 5 more minutes, until lightly golden. Remove from the heat and let cool.

Yield: 3 cups (750 g)

Sautéed Figs

Figs are a natural accompaniment to the Ricotta and Honey Cheesecake (page 40).

4 tablespoons (56 g) unsalted butter

4 tablespoons (80 g) honey

16 Black Mission figs, halved

In a large sauté pan, heat the butter and honey over medium heat, until the butter is completely melted. Whisk together until combined, and then add the figs. Cook for 4 to 5 minutes, until the figs are heated through. Remove from the heat.

Yield: 2 cups (500 g)

Classic Cherry Topping

I like to use Morello cherries, but any tart cherry works well. If fresh aren't available, frozen or jarred are readily found. This is a great topping for the Philadelphia-Style Cheesecake (page 37).

2 tablespoons (30 ml) water

1 tablespoon (8 g) cornstarch

½ cup (100 g) sugar

1 pound (454 g) pitted Morello cherries, drained if using frozen or jarred

In a medium-size saucepan, whisk together the water and cornstarch, making sure the cornstarch is completely dissolved. Whisk in the sugar. Place over medium-high heat and bring to a boil, whisking constantly. Allow to boil for 30 seconds to 1 minute, or until the mixture becomes translucent. Remove from the heat and stir in the cherries. Allow the mixture to cool completely. Pour on top of whole cheesecake, allowing the cherries to drip off the sides.

Yield: 2 cups (500 g)

Pomegranate Glaze

This is for the Israeli Cheesecake (page 46). The deep burgundy color is a stunning contrast to the whiteness of the cheesecake.

2 cups (470 ml) pomegranate juice

2 tablespoons (24 g) sugar

In a medium-size saucepan, combine the pomegranate juice and sugar. Cook over medium heat for about 20 minutes, or until the mixture is syrupy and thickened.

Yield: 1 cup (235 ml)

Candied Orange Peel

This is a perfect garnish for the Cannoli Cheesecake (page 131). Lemons can be substituted for the oranges if you prefer.

4 oranges

1 cup (200 g) sugar

1 cup (235 ml) water

Cut the top and bottom ends off of the oranges. Stand the orange on one of the cut ends and, using a paring knife, begin to cut the peel away in wide strips that are about 2 inches (5 cm) long. Then slice the wide strips into thinner strips, ¼ inch (6 mm) wide by 2 inches (5 cm) long.

Fill a 4-quart (4 L) saucepan halfway with water and bring to a boil; add the orange strips and cook for 5 minutes. Drain and repeat this process. Combine the sugar and water in the saucepan and bring to a boil; add the orange strips and cook for about 5 minutes, until the strips are tender and the liquid is syrupy. Drain and place the strips on a parchment-lined cookie tray to cool to room temperature. Refrigerate until ready to use. Can be refrigerated for up to 2 months.

Yield: 1 cup (240 g)

Apple Cider Reduction

This is optional for the Fennel and Apple Cheesecake (page 84), but it really helps bring out the apple flavor.

2 cups (470 ml) apple cider

In a medium-size saucepan, add the apple cider and cook over medium-high heat for about 30 minutes, or until the mixture is syrupy and thickened.

Yield: 1 cup (235 ml)

Chocolate, Caramel, and Whipped Cream

Chocolate Sauce

This is a basic sauce that can be served with any of the cheesecakes. It is perfect to drizzle over the top of each slice before serving.

8 ounces (228 g) semisweet chocolate, finely chopped

¾ cup (180 ml) heavy cream

1 tablespoon (14 g) unsalted butter

Place the chocolate in a heatproof bowl and set aside. Place the cream in a medium-size saucepan and bring to a boil over medium-high heat. Immediately pour the cream over the chocolate, shake the bowl back and forth for 30 seconds, and allow to stand for 1 minute. Add the butter and whisk just until combined, as not to add too much air to the glaze. Pour over the cheesecake and allow to set until firm.

Yield: 1½ cups (355 ml)

Chocolate Glaze

This glaze is for the Gluten-Free Triple Chocolate Cheesecake (page 60). Make the glaze no more than 1 hour before you plan on glazing the cheesecake.

2 ounces (56 g) chocolate, finely chopped

¼ cup (60 ml) heavy cream

Place the chocolate in a heatproof bowl. Place the cream in a medium-size saucepan and bring to a boil; pour over the chocolate and whisk until smooth. Set aside at room temperature until ready to use.

Yield: ½ cup (120 ml)

Chocolate Shavings or Grated Chocolate

Chocolate shavings are a clean, simple garnish for any cheesecake and are used for the White Chocolate Cheesecake with Cranberry Jewels (page 50), the Gluten-Free Triple Chocolate Cheesecake (page 60), the Tiramisu Cheesecake (page 143), and the Black-Bottom Cheesecake Bars (page 124).

1 block (not bar) of chocolate (white, milk, semi-sweet, or bittersweet)

To make chocolate shavings: Hold the block of chocolate in your hand. You can wrap that part of the block in a small towel or paper towel to avoid melting. Using a vegetable peeler, shave away from you onto parchment paper to get thin, flat chocolate shavings.

To make grated chocolate: Wrap part of the block in a small towel or paper towel to avoid melting. Using a box grater, grate the chocolate onto a sheet of parchment paper.

Whipped Cream

Whipped cream is extremely versatile. You can have it unsweetened or with added sugar. It can also be flavored with a favorite extract or liqueur. This recipe is used for the Blueberry Cheesecake Trifle (page 126), but can also be used as garnish for just about any recipe—just reduce the recipe accordingly for all the others.

1 cup (235 ml) heavy cream

2 tablespoons (26 g) granulated sugar

Place the cream in the bowl of an electric mixer and, using the whip attachment, beat just until stiff peaks are formed.

Yield: 2 cups (470 ml)

Whipped Coconut Cream

This is a great substitute for whipped cream in general, but is a great flavor enhancer for the Buttermilk Chocolate Almond Chia Cheesecake (page 128).

1 can (13.5 ounces, or 400 ml) full-fat coconut milk, chilled overnight in the refrigerator

1 tablespoon (12 g) sugar

1 teaspoon vanilla extract

Scoop the thick solidified cream from the top of the can and place in the bowl of an electric mixer with the whip attachment. Add the sugar and vanilla extract and beat on high speed for about 2 minutes, or until thick and smooth.

Yield: ½ cup (50 g)

Caramel Sauce

This caramel works well with any of the cheesecakes, but goes especially well with the Caramel Apple Crumb Cheesecake (page 70). I also like to add a pinch of black pepper and coarse sea salt for another layer of flavor.

1 cup (200 g) sugar

¼ cup (60 ml) water

4 tablespoons (56 g) unsalted butter

½ cup (120 ml) heavy cream

In a large saucepan, combine the sugar and water and cook over medium-low heat, stirring occasionally, until the sugar has dissolved, 4 to 5 minutes. Increase the heat to high and continue cooking, without stirring, until the caramel is a deep amber color, 6 to 8 minutes. Remove from the heat and carefully add the butter and heavy cream. Whisk until smooth. Allow to cool slightly before serving. Can be stored in the refrigerator for up to 2 weeks. Reheat before serving.

Yield: 1⅓ cups (320 g)

Nuts and Seeds

Candied Walnuts

This is for the Blue Cheese Cheesecake (page 88), but pairs well with any savory cheesecake. Any nuts can be substituted in this recipe. This provides a great textural balance to serve with any of the savory cheesecakes.

3 tablespoons (42 g) unsalted butter

3 tablespoons (45 g) brown sugar

1 cup (160 g) coarsely chopped walnuts

1 teaspoon ground cumin

¼ teaspoon cayenne

In a large sauté pan over medium heat, combine the butter and brown sugar and cook until the butter is melted. Add the walnuts and continue cooking for 3 to 4 minutes, stirring occasionally, until the walnuts are lightly toasted. Add the cumin and cayenne and cook for another minute. Remove from the heat, spread out on a baking sheet, and allow to cool completely.

Yield: 1 cup (160 g)

Nut Brittle

Any nuts can be substituted for the almonds. Macadamia nuts are exceptionally delicious with this. This can be used for the Avocado Cheesecake or the Fennel and Apple Cheesecake (page 63 or 84).

1 cup (200 g) sugar

¼ cup (60 ml) water

2 tablespoons (40 g) honey

2 tablespoons (28 g) unsalted butter

½ teaspoon vanilla extract

¼ teaspoon baking soda

1 cup (160 g) chopped toasted almonds

Combine the sugar, water, and honey in a large saucepan. Cook over medium heat until it reaches 300°F (150°C) (the hard crack stage) on a candy thermometer. Remove from the heat and immediately add the butter, vanilla, baking soda, and almonds. Stir quickly to combine and immediately pour onto buttered cookie sheets. Allow to cool, and then break into pieces.

Yield: 12 ounces (336 g)

VARIATION: FENNEL SEED BRITTLE
Substitute ½ cup (46 g) fennel seeds for the almonds.

Toasted Butternut Squash Seeds

These taste amazing and provide the perfect balance to the Spiced Butternut Squash Cheesecake (page 96). You can use any squash seed for this recipe.

1 cup (240 g) butternut squash seeds

2 teaspoons grapeseed oil

1 teaspoon ground cumin

½ teaspoon ground coriander

½ teaspoon kosher salt

Preheat the oven to 350ºF (180ºC, or gas mark 4).

In a small bowl, toss together the butternut squash seeds, oil, cumin, coriander, and salt. Spread out on a baking sheet and bake for about 15 minutes, or until lightly golden brown. Remove from the oven and allow to cool.

Yield: 1 cup (240 g)

Flavored Oil and Syrup

Herb Oil

This oil, for the White Bean and Herb Cheese-cake (page 94), can be made in advance and stored in the refrigerator for up to 2 weeks. Warm slightly before serving.

1 cup (240 ml) olive oil

4 cloves garlic, peeled and crushed

2 sprigs fresh thyme

1 sprig fresh rosemary

In a medium-size saucepan, heat the olive oil over medium-low heat until just hot to the touch. Remove from the heat and add the garlic, thyme, and rosemary. Allow to infuse for at least 1 hour. Strain out the garlic and herbs before using.

Yield: 1 cup (240 ml)

Rose Syrup

Find the reddest rose petals you can to make this syrup for the Goat Cheese and Rose Cheesecake (page 66), as it will intensify the color. Be sure to use only rose petals that have not been sprayed with pesticides. If you do not have access to fresh rose petals, dried petals are a great substitute and easily available. You can substitute any edible flower, but try to pick ones with bright colors.

FRESH ROSE PETAL SYRUP

1 cup (60 g) packed fresh organic rose petals

1 cup (200 g) sugar, divided

2 cups (470 ml) water

¼ teaspoon vanilla extract

In a medium-size bowl, combine the rose petals and ¼ cup (50 g) of the sugar, rub them together to bruise the petals, then cover and set aside overnight.

In a medium-size saucepan, combine the remaining ¾ cup (150 g) sugar and the water; bring to a boil and then add the rose petal/sugar mixture. Simmer the mixture for about 15 minutes, or until syrupy and thickened. Remove from the heat and allow to cool completely. Strain the syrup and discard the petals. Stir in the vanilla. Refrigerate the syrup until ready to use.

Yield: 1 cup (235 ml)

DRIED ROSE PETAL SYRUP

½ cup (30 g) dried rose petals

2 cups (470 ml) water

1 cup (200 g) sugar

½ teaspoon vanilla extract

In a medium-size bowl, combine the rose petals and water; cover and set aside overnight. Strain the syrup and discard the petals.

In a medium-size saucepan, combine the rose water and sugar; bring to a boil, reduce the heat to a simmer, and cook for about 30 minutes, or until the mixture is syrupy and thickened. Remove from the heat and allow to cool completely. Stir in the vanilla. Refrigerate the syrup until ready to use.

Yield: 1 cup (235 ml)

Acknowledgments

There are many people who worked with me to make this book happen. No words can express the immense gratitude I have for each of you. I truly appreciate your support and dedication not only to the book, but also to me. Thank you.

To my editor, Joy Aquilino, thank you for finding me. Your support, guidance, patience, and trust were immeasurable. To Heather Godin, Betsy Gammons, Katie Fawkes, and Becky Gissel at Quarry Books for your talents, insights, and direction.

To Karen Levy, my copy editor and Kathy Dragolich, my proofreader: You are both amazing.

To Sharon Gutstadt, my friend and talented food stylist: I am so grateful for your friendship.

To photographer extraordinaire Marcus Tullis: You are a gem! Thank you for not only your beautiful work but also your wonderful insights and all of your help with props.

To Rick Smilow, president of the Institute of Culinary Education, for giving me the platform to write this book. To the Stewarding Department for their help, especially Don Mitchell, Jamie Olenick, and Kim Little. To Carmen Serrano for your support and assistance. Special thanks to Kate McCue and Susan Streit Sherman for giving me the opportunity to blossom and allowing me to be me.

To all of my students at ICE: Thank you, thank you, thank you!

To Gretchen Witt Holt, vice president of marketing at OXO, for your generosity.

To Sharon Franke, director of kitchen appliances and technology at *Good Housekeeping*, for your insights into the best cheesecake pans.

To my friends who shared kind words and tastes of cheesecake: Sarah Abrams, Kelley Archer, Christine Beydoun, Stella Cook, Jillian Coulton, Amy D'Amato, James David, Gareth Esersky, Ellen Honig, Anita Jacobson, Carey Jung, Aleena Knight, Jennifer Meier, Anjali Melwani, Mariela Moscoso, Virginia Piotrowski, Ellie Rabinovich, Maureen Shillet, and Cara Tannenbaum.

To Allison Thomas Rodriquez for your friendship, honesty, and never-ending support. Thank you for always listening and being my sounding board.

Special thanks to Nathalie Dupree, Jody Eddy, and Cheryl Sternman Rule for kind words.

To my grandparents, Charlie and Eloise: Thank you for teaching me about food, cooking, and the importance of following your heart.

To my dad, mom, and sisters for your love and support.

To my husband, Amir, and my children, Christian and Alexander: I love you and you are my inspiration.

About the Author

Chef Melanie Underwood developed her enthusiasm for fresh and organic food as a child on her family's farm in Loudoun County, Virginia, where she began cooking at age four. She apprenticed with noted pastry chef Jill Light at a hotel in Washington, D.C. before moving to New York, where she demonstrated her talent for baking and desserts at the Four Seasons Hotel, the Plaza Hotel, Torre di Pisa, and other celebrated New York City restaurants. Since 1996 Underwood has been sharing her expertise as a cooking and baking instructor for professional and recreational programs at the Institute for Culinary Education (ice.edu), has taught private cooking classes at Home Cooking New York in Manhattan's SoHo neighborhood (homecookingny.com), and is

Photo: Institute of Culinary Education

frequently invited to teach throughout the country. Underwood also tests and develops recipes for many corporate clients, including Dairy Management, Diageo, Folgers Coffee, Kraft Foods, Sara Lee, Splenda, Ziploc, and other high-profile brands. She has demonstrated her skills on several TV networks, including NBC ("The Today Show"), ABC ("Live with Regis and Kelly"), CNN, Food Network, and Oxygen, and has been featured in the *New York Times*, the *New York Daily News*, *New York* magazine, *Fine Cooking* magazine, and other publications. Underwood is also a co-author of the self-published book *Art and Cook*, a unique blend of recipes, art, and politics.

Melanie can be reached at Melanieunderwood.com.

Resources

CHEESES I used Philadelphia cream cheese and Vermont Creamery cheeses for the recipes in this book. Vermont Creamery sells crème fraiche, fromage blanc, mascarpone, quark, as well as others. On the TnuvaUSA website, you can search by zip code to find local stores where the Israeli white cheese gvina levana is sold.

www.tnuvausa.com

www.vermontcreamery.com

CHEESECAKE PANS I tested all the recipes using Fat Daddio's and Kuhn Rikon pans. They have push pan and springform pans available.

fatdaddios.com

KuhnRikon.com

surlatable.com

CHERRY BLOSSOM EXTRACT This is often sold as sakura essence.

www.amoretti.com

CHIA SEEDS, DRIED LAVENDER, DRIED ROSE PETALS, TEAS AND TEA POWDERS, HERBS AND SPICES The following stores are well stocked with almost all the herbs, spices, and teas that you need to make all the cheesecakes in this book. Your local options can easily be found online.

Kalustyans
www.kalustyans.com

Mountain Rose Herbs
www.mountainroseherbs.com

Dried Lavender
Bulkherbstore.com

Dried Rose Petals
Bulkherbstore.com

VANILLA BEANS, ESSENCE, AND EXTRACT
Beanilla has a wide variety of vanilla from many countries, but Maui Preserved has some of the only U.S.–grown vanilla beans.

www.beanilla.com

www.mauipreserved.com

Index